The Story of Charles Strange

A Novel.
(Volume III)

Mrs. Henry Wood

Alpha Editions

This edition published in 2024

ISBN : 9789362929198

Design and Setting By
Alpha Editions
www.alphaedis.com
Email - info@alphaedis.com

As per information held with us this book is in Public Domain.
This book is a reproduction of an important historical work. Alpha Editions uses the best technology to reproduce historical work in the same manner it was first published to preserve its original nature. Any marks or number seen are left intentionally to preserve its true form.

Contents

CHAPTER I. ON THE WATCH. .... - 1 -

CHAPTER II. TOM HERIOT. .... - 13 -

CHAPTER III. AN EVENING VISITOR. .... - 21 -

CHAPTER IV. RESTITUTION. .... - 28 -

CHAPTER V. CONFESSION. .... - 39 -

CHAPTER VI. DANGER. .... - 49 -

CHAPTER VII. WITH MR. JONES .... - 57 -

CHAPTER VIII. AN ACCIDENT. .... - 69 -

CHAPTER IX. LAST DAYS. .... - 77 -

CHAPTER X. LAST WORDS. .... - 84 -

CHAPTER XI. DOWN AT MARSHDALE. .... - 94 -

CHAPTER XII. IN THE EAST WING. .... - 103 -

CHAPTER XIII. CONCLUSION. .... - 114 -

CHAPTER I.
ON THE WATCH.

MR. SERJEANT STILLINGFAR sat at dinner in his house in Russell Square one Sunday afternoon. A great cause, in which he was to lead, had brought him up from circuit, to which he would return when the Nisi Prius trial was over. The cloth was being removed when I entered. He received me with his usual kindly welcome.

"Why not have come to dinner, Charles? Just had it, you say? All the more reason why we might have had it together. Sit down, and help yourself to wine."

Declining the wine, I drew my chair near to his, and told him what I had come about.

A few days had gone on since the last chapter. With the trouble connected with Mrs. Brightman, and the trouble connected with Tom Heriot, I had enough on my mind at that time, if not upon my shoulders. As regarded Mrs. Brightman, no one could help me; but regarding the other——

Was Tom in London, or was he not? How was I to find out? I had again gone prowling about the book-stall and its environs, and had seen no trace of him. Had Leah really seen him, or only some other man who resembled him?

Again I questioned Leah. Her opinion was not to be shaken. She held emphatically to her assertion. It was Tom that she had seen, and none other.

"You may have seen some other sailor, sir; I don't say to the contrary; but the sailor I saw was Captain Heriot," she reiterated. "Suppose I go again to-night, sir? I may, perhaps, have the good luck to see him."

"Should you call it good luck, Leah?"

"Ah well, sir, you know what I mean," she answered. "Shall I go to-night?"

"No, Leah; I am going myself. I cannot rest in this uncertainty."

Rest! I felt more like a troubled spirit or a wandering ghost. Arthur Lake asked what had gone wrong with me, and where I disappeared to of an evening.

Once more I turned out in discarded clothes to saunter about Lambeth. It was Saturday night and the thoroughfares were crowded; but amidst all who came and went I saw no trace of Tom.

Worried, disheartened, I determined to carry the perplexity to my Uncle Stillingfar. That he was true as steel, full of loving-kindness to all the world, no matter what their errors, and that he would aid me with his counsel—if any counsel could avail—I well knew. And thus I found myself at his house on that Sunday afternoon. Of course he had heard about the escape of the convicts; had seen Tom's name in the list; but he did not know that he was suspected of having reached London. I told him of what Leah had seen, and added the little episode about "Miss Betsy."

"And now, what can be done, Uncle Stillingfar? I have come to ask you."

His kindly blue eyes became thoughtful whilst he pondered the question. "Indeed, Charles, I know not," he answered. "Either you must wait in patience until he turns up some fine day—as he is sure to do if he is in London—or you must quietly pursue your search for him, and smuggle him away when you have found him."

"But if I don't find him? Do you think it could be Tom that Leah saw? Is it possible that he can be in London?"

"Quite possible. If a homeward vessel, bound, it may be, for the port of London, picked them up, what more likely than that he is here? Again, who else would call himself Charles Strange, and pass himself off for you? Though I cannot see his motive for doing it."

"Did you ever know any man so recklessly imprudent, uncle?"

"I have never known any man so reckless as Tom Heriot. You must do your best to find him, Charles."

"I don't know how. I thought you might possibly have suggested some plan. Every day increases his danger."

"It does: and the chances of his being recognised."

"It seems useless to search further in Lambeth: he must have changed his quarters. And to look about London for him will be like looking for a needle in a bottle of hay. I suppose," I slowly added, "it would not do to employ a detective?"

"Not unless you wish to put him into the lion's mouth," said the Serjeant. "Why, Charles, it would be his business to retake him. Rely upon it, the police are now looking for him if they have the slightest suspicion that he is here."

At that time one or two private detectives had started in business on their own account, having nothing to do with the police: now they have sprung up in numbers. It was to these I alluded.

Serjeant Stillingfar shook his head. "I would not trust one of them, Charles: it would be too dangerous an experiment. No; what you do, you must do yourself. Once let Government get scent that he is here, and we shall probably find the walls placarded with a reward for his apprehension."

"One thing I am surprised at," I said as I rose to leave: "that if he is here, he should not have let me know it. What can he be doing for money? An escaped convict is not likely to have much of that about him."

Serjeant Stillingfar shook his head. "There are points about the affair that I cannot fathom, Charles. Talking of money—you are well-off now, but if more than you can spare should be needed to get Tom Heriot away, apply to me."

"Thank you, uncle; but I don't think it will be needed. Where would you recommend him to escape to?"

"Find him first," was the Serjeant's answer.

He accompanied me himself to the front door. As we stood, speaking a last word, a middle-aged man, with keen eyes and spare frame, dressed as a workman, came up with a brisk step. Mr. Serjeant Stillingfar met the smile on the man's face as he glanced up in passing.

"Arkwright!" he exclaimed. "I hardly knew you. Some sharp case in hand, I conclude?"

"Just so, Serjeant; but I hope to bring it to earth before the day's over. You know——"

Then the man glanced at me and came to a pause.

"However, I mustn't talk about it now, so good-afternoon, Serjeant." And thus speaking, he walked briskly onwards.

"I wonder what he has in hand? I think he would have told me, Charles, but for your being present," cried my uncle, looking after him. "A keen man is Arkwright."

"*Arkwright!*" I echoed, the name now impressing itself upon me. "Surely not Arkwright the famous detective!"

"Yes, it is. And he has evidently got himself up as a workman to further some case that he has in hand. He knew you, Charles; depend upon that; though you did not know him."

A fear, perhaps a foolish one, fell upon me. "Uncle Stillingfar," I breathed, "can his case be *Tom's*? Think you it is he who is being run to earth?"

"No, no. That is not likely," he answered, after a moment's consideration. "Anyway, you must use every exertion to find him, for his stay in London is full of danger."

It will readily be believed that this incident had not added to my peace of mind. One more visit I decided to pay to the old ground in Lambeth, and after that—why, in truth, whether to turn east, west, north or south, I knew no more than the dead.

Monday was bright and frosty; Monday evening clear, cold and starlight. The gaslights flared away in the streets and shops; the roads were lined with wayfarers.

Sauntering down the narrow pavement on the opposite side of the way, in the purposeless manner that a hopeless man favours, I approached the book-stall. A sailor was standing before it, his head bent over the volumes. Every pulse within me went up to fever heat: for there was that in him that reminded me of Tom Heriot.

I crossed quietly to the stall, stood side by side with him, and took up a handful of penny dreadfuls. Yes, it was he—Tom Heriot.

"Tom," I cried softly. "Tom!"

I felt the start he gave. But he did not move hand or foot; only his eyes turned to scan me.

"Tom," I whispered again, apparently intent upon a grand picture of a castle in flames, and a gentleman miraculously escaping with a lady from an attic window. "Tom, don't you know me?"

"For goodness' sake don't speak to me, Charley!" he breathed in answer, the words barely audible. "Go away, for the love of heaven! I've been a prisoner here for the last three minutes. That policeman yonder would know me, and I dare not turn. His name's Wren."

Three doors off, a policeman was standing at the edge of the pavement, facing the shops, as if waiting to pounce upon someone he was expecting to pass. Even as Tom spoke, he wheeled round to the right, and marched up the street. Tom as quickly disappeared to the left, leaving a few words in my ear.

"I'll wait for you at the other end, Charley; it is darker there than here. Don't follow me immediately."

So I remained where I was, still bending an enraptured gaze upon the burning castle and the gallant knight and damsel escaping from it at their peril.

"Betsy says the account comes to seven shillings, Mr. Strange."

The address gave me almost as great a thrill as the sight of Tom had done. It came from the man Lee, now emerging from his shop. Involuntarily I pulled my hat lower upon my brow. He looked up and down the street.

"Oh, I beg pardon—thought Mr. Strange was standing here," he said. And then I saw my error. He had not spoken to me, but to Tom Heriot. My gaze was still fascinated by the flaming picture.

"Anything you'd like this evening, sir?"

"I'll take this sheet—half a dozen of them," I said, putting down sixpence.

"Thank you, sir. A fine night."

"Yes, very. Were you speaking to the sailor who stood here?" I added carelessly "He went off in that direction, I think," pointing to the one opposite to that Tom had taken.

"Yes," answered the man; "'twas Mr. Strange. He had asked me to look how much his score was for tobacco. I dare say he'll be back presently. Captain Strange, by rights," added Lee chattily.

"Oh! Captain of a vessel?"

"Of his own vessel—a yacht. Not but what he has been about the world in vessels of all sorts, he tells us; one voyage before the mast, the next right up next to the skipper. But for them ups and downs where, as he says, would sailors find their experience?"

"Very true. Well, this is all I want just now. Good-evening."

"Good-evening, sir," replied Caleb Lee.

The end of the street to which Tom had pointed was destitute of shops; the houses were small and poor; consequently, it was tolerably dark. Tom was sauntering along, smoking a short pipe.

"Is there any place at hand where we can have a few words together in tolerable security?" I asked.

"Come along," briefly responded Tom. "You walk on the other side of the street, old fellow; keep me in view."

It was good advice, and I took it. He increased his pace to a brisk walk, and presently turned down a narrow passage, which brought him to a sort of small, triangular green, planted with shrubs and trees. I followed, and we sat down on one of the benches.

"Are you quite mad, Tom?"

"Not mad a bit," laughed Tom. "I say, Charley, did you come to that book-stall to look after me?"

"Ay. And it's about the tenth time I have been there."

"How the dickens did you find me out?"

"Chance one evening took Leah into the neighbourhood, and she happened to see you. I had feared you might be in England."

"You had heard of the wreck of the *Vengeance*, I suppose; and that a few of us had escaped. Good old Leah! Did I give her a fright?"

We were sitting side by side. Tom had put his pipe out, lest the light should catch the sight of any passing stragglers. We spoke in whispers. It was, perhaps, as safe a place as could be found; nevertheless, I sat upon thorns.

Not so Tom. By the few signs that might be gathered—his light voice, his gay laugh, his careless manner—Tom felt as happy and secure as if he had been attending one of her Majesty's levées, in the full glory of scarlet coat and flashing sword-blade.

"Do you know, Tom, you have half killed me with terror and apprehension? How could you be so reckless as to come back to London?"

"Because the old ship brought me," lightly returned Tom.

"I suppose a vessel picked you up—and the comrades who escaped with you?"

"It picked two of us up. The other three died."

"What, in the boat?"

He nodded. "In the open boat at sea."

"How did you manage to escape? I thought convicts were too well looked after."

"So they are, under ordinary circumstances. Shipwrecks form the exception. I'll give you the history, Charley."

"Make it brief, then. I am upon thorns."

Tom laughed, and began:

"We were started on that blessed voyage, a cargo of men in irons, and for some time made a fair passage, and thought we must be nearing the other side. Such a crew, that cargo, Charles! Such an awful lot! Villainous wretches, who wore their guilt on their faces, and suffered their deserts; half demons, most of them. A few amongst them were no doubt like me, innocent enough; wrongfully accused and condemned——"

"But go on with the narrative, Tom."

"I swear I was innocent," he cried, with emotion, heedless of my interruption. "I was wickedly careless, I admit that, but the guilt was another's, not mine. When I put those bills into circulation, Charles, I knew no more they were forged than you did. Don't you believe me?"

"I do believe you. I have believed you throughout."

"And if the trial had not been hurried on I think it could have been proved. It was hurried on, Charles, and when it was on it was hurried over. I am suffering unjustly."

"Yes, Tom. But won't you go on with your story?"

"Where was I? Oh, about the voyage and the shipwreck. After getting out of the south-east trades, we had a fortnight's light winds and calms, and then got into a steady westerly wind, before which we ran quietly for some days. One dark night, it was the fifteenth of November, and thick, drizzling weather, the wind about north-west, we had turned in and were in our first sleep, when a tremendous uproar arose on deck; the watch shouting and tramping, the officers' orders and the boatswain's mate's shrill piping rising above the din. One might have thought Old Nick had leaped on board and was giving chase. Next came distinctly that fearful cry, 'All hands save ship!' Sails were being clewed up, yards were being swung round. Before we could realize what it all meant, the ship had run ashore; and there she stuck, bumping as if she would knock her bottom out."

"Get on, Tom," I whispered, for he had paused, and seemed to be spinning a long yarn instead of a short one.

"Fortunately, the ship soon made a sort of cradle for herself in the sand, and lay on her starboard bilge. To attempt to get her off was hopeless. So they got us all out of the ship and on shore, and put us under tents made of the sails. The skipper made out, or thought he made out, the island to be that of Tristan d'Acunha: whether it was or not I can't say positively. At first we thought it was uninhabited, but it turned out to have a few natives on it, sixty or eighty in all. In the course of a few days every movable thing had been landed. All the boats were intact, and were moored in a sort of creek, or small natural harbour, their gear, sails and oars in them."

"Hush!" I breathed, "or you are lost!"

A policeman's bull's-eye was suddenly turned upon the grass. By the man's size, I knew him for Tom's friend, Wren. We sat motionless. The light just escaped us, and the man passed on. But we had been in danger.

"If you would only be quicker, Tom. I don't want to know about boats and their gear."

He laughed. "How impatient you are, Charles! Well, to get on ahead. A cargo of convicts cannot be kept as securely under such circumstances as had befallen us as they could be in a ship's hold, and the surveillance exercised was surprisingly lax. Two or three of the prisoners were meditating an escape, and thought they saw their way to effecting it by means of one of the boats. I found this out, and joined the party. But there were almost insurmountable difficulties in the way. It was absolutely necessary that we should put on ordinary clothes—for what vessel, picking us up, but would have delivered us up at the first port it touched at, had we been in convict dress? We marked the purser's slop-chest, which was under a tent, and well filled, and——"

"Do get on, Tom!"

"Here goes, then! One calm, but dark night, when other people were sleeping, we stole down to the creek, five of us, rigged ourselves out in the purser's toggery, leaving the Government uniforms in exchange, unmoored one of the cutters, and got quietly away. We had secreted some bread and salt meat; water there had been already on board. The wind was off the land, and we let the boat drift before it a bit before attempting to make sail. By daylight we were far enough from the island; no chance of their seeing us—a speck on the waters. The wind, hitherto south, had backed to the westward. We shaped a course by the sun to the eastward, and sailed along at the rate of five or six knots. My comrades were not as rough as they might have been; rather decent fellows for convicts. Two of them were from Essex; had been sentenced for poaching only. Now began our lookout: constantly straining our eyes along the horizon for a sail, but especially astern for an outward-bounder, but only saw one or two in the distance that did not see us. What I underwent in that boat as day after day passed, and no sail appeared, I won't enter upon now, old fellow. The provisions were exhausted, and so was the water. One by one three of my companions went crazy and died. The survivor and I had consigned the last of them to the deep on the twelfth day, and then I thought my turn had come; but Markham was worse than I was. How many hours went on, I knew not. I lay at the bottom of the boat, exhausted and half unconscious, when suddenly I heard voices. I imagined it to be a dream. But in a few minutes a boat was alongside the cutter, and two of its crew had stepped over and were raising me up. They spoke to me, but I was too weak to understand or answer; in fact, I was delirious. I and Markham were taken on board and put to bed. After some days, passed in a sort of dreamy, happy delirium, well cared for and attended to, I woke up to the realities of life. Markham was dead: he had never revived, and died of exposure and weakness some hours after the rescue."

"What vessel had picked you up?"

"It was the *Discovery*, a whaler belonging to Whitby, and homeward bound. The captain, Van Hoppe, was Dutch by birth, but had been reared in England and had always sailed in English ships. A good and kind fellow, if ever there was one. Of course, I had to make my tale good and suppress the truth. The passenger-ship in which I was sailing to Australia to seek my fortune had foundered in mid-ocean, and those who escaped with me had died of their sufferings. That was true so far. Captain Van Hoppe took up my misfortunes warmly. Had he been my own brother—had he been *you*, Charley—he could not have treated me better or cared for me more. The vessel had a prosperous run home. She was bound for the port of London; and when I put my hand into Van Hoppe's at parting, and tried to thank him for his goodness, he left a twenty-pound note in it. 'You'll need it, Mr. Strange,' he said; 'you can repay me when your fortune's made and you are rich.'"

"*Strange!*" I cried.

Tom laughed.

"I called myself 'Strange' on the whaler. Don't know that it was wise of me. One day when I was getting better and lay deep in thought—which just then chanced to be of you, Charley—the mate suddenly asked me what my name was. 'Strange,' I answered, on the spur of the moment. That's how it was. And that's the brief history of my escape."

"You have had money, then, for your wants since you landed," I remarked.

"I have had the twenty pounds. It's coming to an end now."

"You ought not to have come to London. You should have got the captain to put you ashore somewhere, and then made your escape from England."

"All very fine to talk, Charley! I had not a sixpence in my pocket, or any idea that he was going to help me. I could only come on as far as the vessel would bring me."

"And suppose he had not given you money—what then?"

"Then I must have contrived to let you know that I was home again, and borrowed from you," he lightly replied.

"Well, your being here is frightfully dangerous."

"Not a bit of it. As long as the police don't suspect I am in England, they won't look after me. It's true that a few of them might know me, but I do not think they would in this guise and with my altered face."

"You were afraid of one to-night."

"Well, *he* is especially one who might know me; and he stood there so long that I began to think he might be watching me. Anyway, I've been on shore these three weeks, and nothing has come of it yet."

"What about that young lady named Betsy? Miss Betsy Lee."

Tom threw himself back in a fit of laughter.

"I hear the old fellow went down to Essex Street one night to ascertain whether I lived there! The girl asked me one day where I lived, and I rapped out Essex Street."

"But, Tom, what have you to do with the girl?"

"Nothing; nothing. On my honour. I have often been in the shop, sometimes of an evening. The father has invited me to some grog in the parlour behind it, and I have sat there for an hour chatting with him and the girl. That's all. She is a well-behaved, modest little girl; none better."

"Well, Tom, with one imprudence and another, you stand a fair chance——"

"There, there! Don't preach, Charley. What you call imprudence, I call fun."

"What do you think of doing? To remain on here for ever in this disguise?"

"Couldn't, I expect, if I wanted to. I must soon see about getting away."

"You must get away at once."

"I am not going yet, Charley; take my word for that; and I am as safe in London, I reckon, as I should be elsewhere. Don't say but I may have to clear out of this particular locality. If that burly policeman is going to make a permanent beat of it about here, he might drop upon me some fine evening."

"And you must exchange your sailor's disguise, as you call it, for a better one."

"Perhaps so. That rough old coat you have on, Charley, might not come amiss to me."

"You can have it. Why do you fear that policeman should know you, more than any other?"

"He was present at the trial last August. Was staring me in the face most of the day. His name's Wren."

I sighed.

"Well, Tom, it is getting late; we have sat here as long as is consistent with safety," I said, rising.

He made me sit down again.

"The later the safer, perhaps, Charley. When shall we meet again?"

"Ay; when, and where?"

"Come to-morrow evening, to this same spot. It is as good a one as any I know of. I shall remain indoors all day tomorrow. Of course one does not care to run needlessly into danger. Shall you find your way to it?"

"Yes, and will be here; but I shall go now. Do be cautious, Tom. Do you want any money? I have brought some with me."

"Many thanks, old fellow; I've enough to go on with for a day or two. How is Blanche? Did she nearly die of the disgrace?"

"She did not know of it. Does not know it yet."

"No!" he exclaimed in astonishment. "Why, how can it have been kept from her? She does not live in a wood."

"Level has managed it, somehow. She was abroad during the trial, you know. They have chiefly lived there since, Blanche seeing no English newspapers; and, of course, her acquaintances do not gratuitously speak to her about it. But I don't think it can be kept from her much longer."

"But where does she think I am—all this time?"

"She thinks you are in India with the regiment."

"I suppose *he* was in a fine way about it!"

"Level? Yes—naturally; and is still. He would have saved you, Tom, at any cost."

"As you would, and one or two more good friends; but, you see, I did not know what was coming upon me in time to ask them. It fell upon my head like a thunderbolt. Level is not a bad fellow at bottom."

"He is a downright good one—at least, that's my opinion of him."

We stood hand locked in hand at parting. "Where are you staying?" I whispered.

"Not far off. I've a lodging in the neighbourhood—one room."

"Fare you well, then, until to-morrow evening."

"Au revoir, Charley."

CHAPTER II.
TOM HERIOT.

I FOUND my way straight enough the next night to the little green with its trees and shrubs. Tom was there, and was humming one of our boyhood's songs taught us by Leah:

"Young Henry was as brave a youth
As ever graced a martial story;
And Jane was fair as lovely truth:
She sighed for love, and he for glory.

"To her his faith he meant to plight,
And told her many a gallant story:
But war, their honest joys to blight,
Called him away from love to glory.

"Young Henry met the foe with pride;
Jane followed—fought—ah! hapless story!
In man's attire, by Henry's side,
She died for love, and he for glory."

He was still dressed as a sailor, but the pilot-coat was buttoned up high and tight about his throat, and the round glazed hat was worn upon the front of his head instead of the back of it.

"I thought you meant to change these things, Tom," I said as we sat down.

"All in good time," he answered; "don't quite know yet what costume to adopt. Could one become a negro-melody man, think you, Charley—or a Red Indian juggler with balls and sword-swallowing?"

How light he seemed! how supremely indifferent! Was it real or only assumed? Then he turned suddenly upon me:

"I say, what are you in black for, Charley? For my sins?"

"For Mr. Brightman."

"Mr. Brightman!" he repeated, his tone changing to one of concern. "Is he dead?"

"He died the last week in February. Some weeks ago now. Died quite suddenly."

"Well, well, well!" softly breathed Tom Heriot. "I am very sorry. I did not know it. But how am I likely to know anything of what the past months have brought forth?"

It would serve no purpose to relate the interview of that night in detail. We spent it partly in quarrelling. That is, in differences of opinion. It was impossible to convince Tom of his danger. I told him about the Sunday incident, when Detective Arkwright passed the door of Serjeant Stillingfar, and my momentary fear that he might be looking after Tom. He only laughed. "Good old Uncle Stillingfar!" cried he; "give my love to him." And all his conversation was carried on in the same light strain.

"But you must leave Lambeth," I urged. "You said you would do so."

"I said I might. I will, if I see just cause for doing so. Plenty of time yet. I am not *sure*, you know, Charles, that Wren would know me."

"The very fact of your having called yourself 'Strange' ought to take you away from here."

"Well, I suppose that was a bit of a mistake," he acknowledged. "But look here, brother mine, your own fears mislead you. Until it is known that I have made my way home no one will be likely to look after me. Believing me to be at the antipodes, they won't search London for me."

"They may suspect that you are in London, if they don't actually know it."

"Not they. To begin with, it must be a matter of absolute uncertainty whether we got picked up at all, after escaping from the island; but the natural conclusion will be that, if we were, it was by a vessel bound for the colonies: homeward-bound ships do not take that course. Everyone at all acquainted with navigation knows that. I assure you, our being found by the whaler was the merest chance in the world. Be at ease, Charley. I can take care of myself, and I will leave Lambeth if necessary. One of these fine mornings you may get a note from me, telling you I have emigrated to the Isle of Dogs, or some such enticing quarter, and have become 'Mr. Smith.' Meanwhile, we can meet here occasionally."

"I don't like this place, Tom. It must inevitably be attended with more or less danger. Had I not better come to your lodgings?"

"No," he replied, after a moment's consideration. "I am quite sure that we are safe here, and there it's hot and stifling—a dozen families living in the same house. And I shall not tell you where the lodgings are, Charles: you might be swooping down upon me to carry me away as Mephistopheles carried away Dr. Faustus."

After supplying him with money, with a last handshake, whispering a last injunction to be cautious, I left the triangle, and left him within it. The next moment found me face to face with the burly frame and wary glance of Mr. Policemen Wren. He was standing still in the starlight. I walked past him with as much unconcern as I could muster. He turned to look after me for a time, and then continued his beat.

It gave me a scare. What would be the result if Tom met him unexpectedly as I had done? I would have given half I was worth to hover about and ascertain. But I had to go on my way.

"Can you see Lord Level, sir?"

It was the following Saturday afternoon, and I was just starting for Hastings. The week had passed in anxious labour. Business cares for me, more work than I knew how to get through, for Lennard was away ill, and constant mental torment about Tom. I took out my watch before answering Watts.

"Yes, I have five minutes to spare. If that will be enough for his lordship," I added, laughing, as we shook hands: for he had followed Watts into the room.

"You are off somewhere, Charles?"

"Yes, to Hastings. I shall be back again to-morrow night. Can I do anything for you?"

"Nothing," replied Lord Level. "I came up from Marshdale this morning, and thought I would come round this afternoon to ask whether you have any news."

When Lord Level went to Marshdale on the visit that bore so suspicious an aspect to his wife, he had remained there only one night, returning to London the following day. This week he had been down again, and stayed rather longer—two days, in fact. Blanche, as I chanced to know, was rebelling over it. Secretly rebelling, for she had not brought herself to accuse him openly.

"News?" I repeated.

"Of Tom Heriot."

Should I tell Lord Level? Perhaps there was no help for it. When he had asked me before I had known nothing positively; now I knew only too much.

"Why I should have it, I know not; but a conviction lies upon me that he has found his way back to London," he continued. "Charles, you look conscious. Do you know anything?"

"You are right. He is here, and I have seen him."

"Good heavens!" exclaimed Lord Level, throwing himself back in his chair. "Has he really been mad enough to come back to London?"

Drawing my own chair nearer to him, I bent forward, and in low tones gave him briefly the history. I had seen Tom on the Monday and Tuesday nights, as already related to the reader. On the Thursday night I was again at the trysting-place, but Tom did not meet me. The previous night, Friday, I had gone again, and again Tom did not appear.

"Is he taken, think you?" cried Lord Level.

"I don't know: and you see I dare not make any inquiries. But I think not. Had he been captured, it would be in the papers."

"I am not so sure of that. What an awful thing! What suspense for us all! Can *nothing* be done?"

"Nothing," I answered, rising, for my time was up. "We can only wait, and watch, and be silent."

"If it were not for the disgrace reflected upon us, and raking it up again to people's minds, I would say let him be re-taken! It would serve him right for his foolhardiness."

"How is Blanche?"

"Cross and snappish; unaccountably so: and showing her temper to me rather unbearably."

I laughed—willing to treat the matter lightly. "She does not care that you should go travelling without her, I take it."

Lord Level, who was passing out before me, turned and gazed into my face.

"Yes," said he emphatically. "But a man may have matters to take up his attention, and his movements also, that he may deem it inexpedient to talk of to his wife."

He spoke with a touch of haughtiness. "Very true," I murmured, as we shook hands and went out together, he walking away towards Gloucester Place, I jumping into the cab waiting to take me to the station.

Mrs. Brightman was better; I knew that; and showing herself more self-controlled. But there was no certainty that the improvement would be lasting. In truth, the certainty lay rather the other way. Her mother's home was no home for Annabel; and I had formed the resolution to ask her to come to mine.

The sun had set when I reached Hastings, and Miss Brightman's house. Miss Brightman, who seemed to grow less strong day by day, which I was grieved to hear, was in her room lying down. Annabel sat at the front drawing-room window in the twilight. She started up at my entrance, full of surprise and apprehension.

"Oh, Charles! Has anything happened? Is mamma worse?"

"No, indeed; your mamma is very much better," said I cheerfully. "I have taken a run down for the pleasure of seeing you, Annabel."

She still looked uneasy. I remembered the dreadful tidings I had brought the last time I came to Hastings. No doubt she was thinking of it, too, poor girl.

"Take a seat, Charles," she said. "Aunt Lucy will soon be down."

I drew a chair opposite to her, and talked for a little time on indifferent topics. The twilight shades grew deeper, passers-by more indistinct, the sea less bright and shimmering. Silence stole over us—a sweet silence all too conscious, all too fleeting. Annabel suddenly rose, stood at the window, and made some slight remark about a little boat that was nearing the pier.

"Annabel," I whispered, as I rose and stood by her, "you do not know what I have really come down for."

"No," she answered, with hesitation.

"When I last saw you at your own home, you may remember that you were in very great trouble. I asked you to share it with me, but you would not do so."

She began to tremble, and became agitated, and I passed my arm round her waist.

"My darling, I now know all."

Her heart beat violently as I held her. Her hand shook nervously in mine.

"You cannot know all!" she cried piteously.

"I know all; more than you do. Mrs. Brightman was worse after you left, and Hatch sent for me. She and Mr. Close have told me the whole truth."

Annabel would have shrunk away, in the full tide of shame that swept over her, and a low moan broke from her lips.

"Nay, my dear, instead of shrinking from me, you must come nearer to me—for ever. My home must be yours now."

She did not break away from me, and stood pale and trembling, her hands clasped, her emotion strong.

"It cannot, must not be, Charles."

"Hush, my love. It *can* be—and shall be."

"Charles," she said, her very lips trembling, "weigh well what you are saying. Do not suffer the—affection—I must speak fully—the implied engagement that was between us, ere this unhappiness came to my knowledge and yours—do not suffer it to bind you now. It is a fearful disgrace to attach to my poor mother, and it is reflected upon me."

"Were your father living, Annabel, should you say the disgrace was also reflected upon *him*?"

"Oh no, no. I could not do so. My good father! honourable and honoured. Never upon him."

I laughed a little at her want of logic.

"Annabel, my dear, you have yourself answered the question. As I hold you to my heart now, so will I, in as short a time as may be, hold you in my home and at my hearth. Let what will betide, you shall have one true friend to shelter and protect you with his care and love for ever and for ever."

Her tears were falling.

"Oh please, please, Charles! I am sure it ought not to be. Aunt Lucy would tell you so."

Aunt Lucy came in at that moment, and proved to be on my side. She would be going to Madeira at the close of the summer, and the difficulty as to what was to be done then with Annabel had begun to trouble her greatly.

"I cannot take her with me, you see, Charles," she said. "In her mother's precarious state, the child must not absent herself from England. Still less can I leave her to her mother's care. Therefore I think your proposal exactly meets the dilemma. I suppose matters have been virtually settled between you for some little time now."

"Oh, Aunt Lucy!" remonstrated Annabel, blushing furiously.

"Well, my dear, and I say it is all for the best. If you can suggest a better plan I am willing to hear it."

Annabel sat silent, her head drooping.

"I may tell you this much, child: your father looked forward to it and approved it. Not that he would have allowed the marriage to take place just yet had he lived; I am sure of that; but he is not living, and circumstances alter cases."

"I am sure he liked me, Miss Brightman," I ventured to put in, as modestly as I could; "and I believe he would have consented to our marriage."

"Yes, he liked you very much; and so do I," she added, laughing. "I wish I could say as much for Mrs. Brightman. The opposition, I fancy, will come from her."

"You think she will oppose it?" I said—and, indeed, the doubt had lain in my own mind.

"I am afraid so. Of course there will be nothing for it but patience. Annabel cannot marry without her consent."

How a word will turn the scales of our hopes and fears! That Mrs. Brightman would oppose and wither our bright prospects came to me in that moment with the certainty of conviction.

"Come what come may, we will be true to each other," I whispered to Annabel the next afternoon. We were standing at the end of the pier, looking out upon the calm sea, flashing in the sunshine, and I imprisoned her hand momentarily in mine. "If we have to exercise all the patience your Aunt Lucy spoke of, we will still hope on, and put our trust in Heaven."

"Even so, Charles." The evening was yet early when I reached London, and I walked home from the station. St. Mary's was striking half-past seven as I passed it. At the self-same moment, an arm was inserted into mine. I turned quickly, wondering if anyone had designs upon my small hand-bag.

"All right, Charley! I'm not a burglar."

It was only Lake. "Why, Arthur! I thought you had gone to Oxford until Monday!"

"Got news last night that the fellow could not have me: had to go down somewhere or other," he answered, as we walked along arm-in-arm. "I say, I had a bit of a scare just now."

"In what way?"

"I thought I saw Tom pass. Tom Heriot," he added in a whisper.

"Oh, but that's impossible, you know, Lake," I said, though I felt my pulses quicken. "All your fancy."

"It was just under that gas-lamp at the corner of Wellington Street," Lake went on. "He was sauntering along as if he had nothing to do, muffled in a coat that looked a mile too big for him, and a red comforter. He lifted his face in passing, and stopped suddenly, as if he had recognised me, and were going to speak; then seemed to think better of it, turned on his heel and walked back the way he had been coming. Charley, if it was not Tom Heriot, I never saw such a likeness as that man bore to him."

My lips felt glued. "It could not have been Tom Heriot, Lake. You know Tom is at the antipodes. We will not talk of him, please. Are you coming home with me?"

"Yes. I was going on to Barlow's Chambers, but I'll come with you instead."

CHAPTER III.
AN EVENING VISITOR.

THE spring flowers were showing themselves, and the may was budding in the hedges. I thought how charming it all looked, as I turned, this Monday afternoon, into Mrs. Brightman's grounds, where laburnums drooped their graceful blossoms, and lilacs filled the air with their perfume; how significantly it all spoke to the heart of renewed life after the gloom of winter, the death and decay of nature.

Mrs. Brightman was herself, enjoying the spring-tide. She sat, robed in crape, on a bench amidst the trees, on which the sun was shining. What a refined, proud, handsome face was hers! but pale and somewhat haggard now. No other trace of her recent illness was apparent, except a nervous trembling of the hands.

"This is a surprise," she said, holding out one of those hands to me quite cordially. "I thought you had been too busy of late to visit me in the day-time."

"Generally I am very busy, but I made time to come to-day. I have something of importance to say to you, Mrs. Brightman. Will you hear me?"

She paused to look at me—a searching, doubtful look. Did she fear that I was about to speak to her of her *failing*? The idea occurred to me.

"Certainly," she coldly replied. "Business must, of course, be attended to. Would you prefer to go indoors or to sit out here?"

"I would rather remain here. I am not often favoured with such a combination of velvet lawn and sunshine and sweet scents."

She made room for me beside her. And, with as little circumlocution as possible, I brought out what I wanted—Annabel. When the heart is truly engaged, a man at these moments can only be bashful, especially when he sees it will be an uphill fight; but if the heart has nothing to do with the matter, he can be as cool and suave as though he were merely telling an everyday story.

Mrs. Brightman, hearing me to the end, rose haughtily.

"Surely you do not know what you are saying!" she exclaimed. "Or is it that I fail to understand you? You cannot be asking for the hand of my daughter?"

"Indeed—pardon me—I am. Mrs. Brightman, we——"

"Pardon *me*," she interrupted, "but I must tell you that it is utterly preposterous. Say no more, Mr. Strange; not another word. My daughter cannot marry a professional man. *I* did so, you may reply: yes, and have forfeited my proper place in the world ever since."

"Mr. Brightman would have given Annabel to me."

"Possibly so, though I think not. As Mr. Brightman is no longer here, we may let that supposition alone. And you must allow me to say this much, sir—that it is scarcely seemly to come to me on any such subject so soon after his death."

"But——" I stopped in embarrassment, unable to give my reason for speaking so soon. How could I tell Mrs. Brightman that it was to afford Annabel a home and a protector: that this, her mother's home, was not fitting for a refined and sensitive girl?

But I pressed the suit. I told her I had Annabel's consent, and that I had recently been with her at Hastings. I should like to have added that I had Miss Brightman's, only that it might have done more harm than good. I spoke very slightly of Miss Brightman's projected departure from England, when her house would be shut up and Annabel must leave Hastings. And I added that I wanted to make a home for her by that time.

I am sure she caught my implied meaning, for she grew agitated and her hands shook as they lay on her crape dress. Her diamond rings, which she had not discarded, flashed in the sunlight. But she rallied her strength. All her pride rose up in rebellion.

"My daughter has her own home, sir; her home with me—what do you mean? During my illness, I have allowed her to remain with her aunt, but she will shortly return to me."

And when I would have urged further, and pleaded as for something dearer than life, she peremptorily stopped me.

"I will hear no more, Mr. Strange. My daughter is descended on my side from the nobles of the land—you must forgive me for thus alluding to it—and it is impossible that I can forget that, or allow her to do so. Never, with my consent, will she marry out of that grade: a professional man is, in rank, beneath her. This is my decision, and it is unalterable. The subject is at an end, and I beg of you never again to enter upon it."

There was no chance of my pursuing it then, at any rate. Hatch came from the house, a folded cloak on her arm, and approached her mistress.

"The carriage is at the gate, ma'am."

Mrs. Brightman rose at once: she was going for a drive. After what had just passed, I held out my arm to her with some hesitation. She put the tips of her fingers within it, with a stiff "Thank you," and we walked to the gate in silence. I handed her into the open carriage; Hatch disposed the cloak upon her knees, assisted by the footman. With a cold bow, Mrs. Brightman, who had already as coldly shaken hands with me, drove away.

Hatch, always ready for a gossip, stood within the little iron gate while she spoke to me.

"We be going away for a bit, sir," she began. "Did you know it?"

"No. Mrs. Brightman has not mentioned the matter to me."

"Well, we be, then," continued Hatch; "missis and me and Perry. Mr. Close have got her to consent at last. I don't say that she was well enough to go before; Close thought so, but I didn't. He wants her gone, you see, Mr. Charles, to get that fancy out of her head about master."

"But does she still think she sees him?"

"Not for the past few days," replied Hatch. "She has changed her bedroom, and taken to the best spare one; and she has been better in herself. Oh, she'll be all right now for a bit, if only———"

"If only what?" I asked, for Hatch had paused.

"Well, you know, sir. If only she can control herself. I'm certain she is trying to," added Hatch. "There ain't one of us would be so glad to find it got rid of for good and all as she'd be. She's put about frightfully yet at Miss Annabel's knowing of it."

"And where is it that you are going to?"

"Missis talked of Cheltenham; it was early, she thought, for the seaside; but this morning she got a Cheltenham newspaper up, and saw that amid the company staying there were Captain and Lady Grace Chantrey. 'I'm not going where my brother and that wife of his are,' she says to me in a temper—for, as I dare say you've heard, Mr. Charles, they don't agree. And now she talks of Brighton. Whatever place she fixes on, Perry is to be sent on first to take lodgings."

"Well, Hatch," I said, "the change from home will do your mistress good. She is much better. I trust the improvement will be permanent."

"Ah, if she would but take care! It all lies in that, sir," concluded Hatch, as I turned away from the gate, and she went up the garden.

We must go back for a moment to the previous evening. Leaving behind us the church of St. Clement Danes and its lighted windows, Lake and I turned into Essex Street, arm-in-arm, went down it and reached my door. I opened it with my latch-key. The hall-lamp was not lighted, and I wondered at Watts's neglect.

"Go on up to my room," I said to Lake. "I'll follow you in a moment."

He bounded up the stairs, and the next moment Leah came up from the kitchen with a lighted candle, her face white and terrified.

"It is only myself, Leah. Why is the lamp not alight?"

"Heaven be good to us, sir!" she cried. "I thought I heard somebody go upstairs."

"Mr. Lake has gone up."

She dropped her candlestick upon the slab, and backed against the wall, looking more white and terrified than ever. I thought she was about to faint.

"Mr. Charles! I feel as if I could die! I ought to have bolted the front door."

"But what for?" I cried, intensely surprised. "What on earth is the matter, Leah?"

"He is up there, sir! Up in your front sitting-room. I put out the hall-lamp, thinking the house would be best in darkness."

"Who is up there?" For in the moment's bewilderment I did not glance at the truth.

"Mr. Tom, sir. Captain Heriot."

"*Mr. Tom!* Up there?"

"Not many minutes ago, soon after Watts had gone out to church—for he was late to-night—there came a ring at the doorbell," said Leah. "I came up to answer it, thinking nothing. A rough-looking man stood, in a wide-awake hat, close against the door there. 'Is Mr. Strange at home?' said he, and walked right in. I knew his voice, and I knew him, and I cried out. 'Don't be stupid, Leah; it's only me,' says he. 'Is Mr. Charles upstairs? Nobody with him, I hope.' 'There's nobody to come and put his head in the lion's mouth, as may be said, there at all, sir,' said I; and up he went, like a lamplighter. I put the hall-lamp out. I was terrified out of my senses, and told him you were at Hastings, but I expected you in soon. And Mr. Charles," wound up Leah, "I think he must have gone clean daft."

"Light the lamp again," I replied. "It always *is* alight, you know. If the house is in darkness, you might have a policeman calling to know what was the matter."

Tom was in a fit of laughter when I got upstairs. He had taken off his rough overcoat and broad-brimmed hat, and stood in a worn—very much worn—suit of brown velveteen breeches and gaiters. Lake stared at him over the table, a comical expression on his face.

"Suppose we shake hands, to begin with," said Lake. And they clasped hands heartily across the table.

"Did you know me just now, in the Strand, Lake?" asked Tom Heriot.

"I did," replied Lake, and his tone proved that he meant it. "I said to Charley, here, that I had just seen a fellow very like Tom Heriot; but I knew who it was, fast enough."

"You wouldn't have known me, though, if I hadn't lifted my face to the lamp-light. I forget myself at moments, you see," added Tom, after a pause. "Meeting you unexpectedly, I was about to speak as in the old days, and recollected myself only just in time. I say"—turning himself about in his velveteens—"should you take me for a gamekeeper?"

"No, I should not: you don't look the thing at all," I put in testily, for I was frightfully vexed with him altogether. "I thought you must have been taken up by your especial friend, Wren. Twice have I been to the trysting-place as agreed, but you did not appear."

"No; but I think he nearly had me," replied Tom.

"How was that?"

"I'll tell you," he answered, as we all three took chairs round the fire, and I stirred it into a blaze. "On the Wednesday I did not go out at all; I told you I should not. On the Thursday, after dusk, I went out to meet you, Charley. It was early, and I strolled in for a smoke with Lee and a chat with Miss Betsy. The old man began at once: 'Captain Strange, Policeman Wren has been here, asking questions about you.' It seems old Wren is well known in the neighbourhood——"

"Captain Strange?" cried Lake. "Who is Captain Strange?"

"I am—down there," laughed Tom. "Don't interrupt, please. 'What questions?' I said to Lee. 'Oh, what your name was, and where you came from, and if I had known you long, and what your ship was called,' answered Lee. 'And you told him?' I asked. 'Well, I should have told him, but for Betsy,' he said. 'Betsy spoke up, saying you were a sailor-gentleman that came in to buy tobacco and newspapers; and that was all he got out of us, not your name, captain, or anything. As Betsy said to me afterwards, it was not our place to answer questions about Captain Strange: if the policeman wanted to know anything, let him apply to the captain himself. Which I thought good sense,' concluded Lee. As it was."

"Well, Tom?"

"Well, I thought it about time to go straight home again," said Tom; "and that's why I did not meet you, Charley. And the next day, Friday, I cleared out of my diggings in that quarter of the globe, rigged myself out afresh, and found other lodgings. I am nearer to you now, Charley: vegetating in the wilds over Blackfriars Bridge."

"How could you be so imprudent as to come here to-night? or to be seen in so conspicuous a spot as the Strand?"

"The fit took me to pay you a visit, old fellow. As to the Strand—it is a fine thoroughfare, you know, and I had not set eyes on it since last summer. I walked up and down a bit, listening to the church bells, and looking about me."

"You turn everything into ridicule, Tom."

"Better that, Charley, than into sighing and groaning."

"How did you know that Leah would open the door to you? Watts might have done so."

"I had it all cut-and-dried. 'Is Mrs. Brown at home?' I should have said, in a voice Watts would never have known. 'Mrs. Brown don't live here,' old Watts would have answered; upon which I should have politely begged his pardon and walked off."

"All very fine, Tom, and you may think yourself amazingly clever; but as sure as you are living, you will run these risks once too often."

"Not I. Didn't I give old Leah a scare! You should have heard her shriek."

"Suppose it had been some enemy—some stickler for law and justice—that I had brought home with me to-night, instead of Lake?"

"But it wasn't," laughed Tom. "It was Lake himself. And I guess he is as safe as you are."

"Be sure of that," added Lake. "But what do you think of doing, Heriot? You cannot hide away for ever in the wilds of Blackfriars. *I* would not answer for your safety there for a day."

"Goodness knows!" said Tom. "Perhaps Charley could put me up here—in one of his top bedrooms?"

Whether he spoke in jest or earnest, I knew not. He might remember that I was running a risk in concealing him even for an hour or two. Were it discovered, the law might make me answer for it.

"I should like something to eat, Charley."

Leaving him with Lake, I summoned Leah, and bade her bring up quickly what she had. She speedily appeared with the tray.

"Good old Leah!" said Tom to her. "That ham looks tempting."

"Mr. Tom, if you go on like this, loitering in the open streets and calling at houses, trouble will overtake you," returned Leah, in much the same tone she had used to reprimand him when a child. "I wonder what your dear, good mother would say to it if she saw you throwing yourself into peril. Do you remember, sir, how often she would beg of you to be good?"

"My mother!" repeated Tom, who was in one of his lightest moods. "Why, you never saw her. She was dead and buried and gone to heaven before you knew anything of us."

"Ah well, Master Tom, you know I mean Mrs. Heriot—afterwards Mrs. Strange. It wouldn't be you, sir, if you didn't turn everything into a jest. She was a good mother to you all."

"That she was, Leah. Excused our lessons for the asking, and fed us on jam."

He was taking his supper rapidly the while; for, of course, he had to be away before church was over and Watts was home again. The man might have been true and faithful; little doubt of it; but it would have added one more item to the danger.

Lake went out and brought a cab; and Tom, his wide-awake low on his brow, his rough coat on, and his red comforter round about his throat, vaulted into it, to be conveyed over Blackfriars Bridge to any point that he might choose to indicate.

"It is an amazing hazard his going about like this," cried Lake, as we sat down together in front of the fire. "He must be got out of England as quickly as possible."

"But he won't go."

"Then, mark my words, Charles, bad will come of it."

CHAPTER IV.
RESTITUTION.

TIME had gone on—weeks and weeks—though there is little to tell of passing events. Things generally remained pretty much as they had been. The Levels were abroad again. Mrs. Brightman on the whole was better, but had occasional relapses; Annabel spent most of her time at Hastings; and Tom Heriot had not yet been taken.

Tom was now at an obscure fishing village on the coast of Scotland, passing himself off as a fisherman, owning a small boat and pretending to fish. This did not allay our anxiety, which was almost as great as ever. Still, it was something to have him away from London. Out of Great Britain he refused to move.

Does the reader remember George Coney's money, that so strangely disappeared the night of Mr. Brightman's death? From that hour to this nothing has been seen or heard of it: but the time for it was now at hand. And what I am about to relate may appear a very common-place ending to a mystery—though, indeed, it was not yet quite the ending. In my capacity of story-teller I could have invented a hundred romantic incidents, and worked them and the reader up to a high point of interest; but I can only record the incident as it happened, and its termination was a very matter-of-fact one.

I was sitting one evening in the front room: a sitting-room now—I think this has been said before—smoking my after-dinner cigar. The window was open to the summer air, which all day long had been intensely hot. A letter received in the morning from Gloucestershire from Mr. Coney, to which his son had scrawled a postscript: "Has that bag turned up yet?" had set me thinking of the loss, and from that I fell to thinking of the loss of the Clavering will, which had followed close upon it. Edmund Clavering, by the way, had been with me that day to impart some news. He was going to be married—to a charming girl, too—and we were discussing settlements. My Lady Clavering, he said, was figuring at Baden-Baden, and report ran that she was about to espouse a French count with a fierce moustache.

Presently I took up the *Times*, not opened before that day, and was deep in a police case, which had convulsed the court in Marlborough Street with laughter, and was convulsing me, when a vehicle dashed down Essex Street. It was the van of the Parcels Delivery Company.

"Mr. Strange live here?" was the question I heard from the man who had descended from the seat beside the driver, when Watts went out.

"All right," said Watts.

"Here's a parcel for him. Nothing to pay."

The driver whipped up his horse, then turned sharply round, and—overturned the van. It was not the first accident of a similar nature, or the last by many, that I have seen in that particular spot. How it is I don't know, but drivers, especially cabmen, have an unconquerable propensity for pulling their horses round in a perilously short fashion at the bottom of Essex Street, and sometimes the result is that they come to grief. I threw down my newspaper and leaned out at the window watching the fun. The street was covered with parcels, and the driver and his friend were throwing off their consternation in choice language. One hamper could not be picked up: it had contained wine loosely packed, and the broken bottles were lying in a red pool. Where the mob collected from, that speedily arrived to assist, was a marvel. The van at length took its departure up the street, considerably shorn of the triumph with which it had dashed down.

This had taken up a considerable space of time, and it was growing too dark to resume my newspaper. Turning from the window, I proceeded to examine the parcel which Watts had brought up on its arrival and placed on the table. It was about a foot square, wrapped in brown paper, sealed and tied with string; and, in what Tony Lumpkin would have called a confounded cramped, up-and-down hand, where you could not tell an izzard from an R, was directed "C. Strange, Esquire."

I took out my penknife, cut the string, and removed the paper; and there was disclosed a pasteboard-box with green edges, also sealed. I opened it, and from a mass of soft paper took out a small canvas bag, tied round with tape, and containing thirty golden sovereigns!

From the very depth of my conviction I believed it to be the bag we had lost. It was the bag; for, on turning it round, there were Mr. Coney's initials, S. C., neatly marked with blue cotton, as they had been on the one left by George. It was one of their sample barley bags. I wondered if they were the same sovereigns. Where had it been? Who had taken it? And who had returned it?

I rang the bell, and then called to Watts, who was coming up to answer it, to bring Leah also. It was my duty to tell them, especially Leah, of the money's restitution, as they had been inmates of the house when it was lost.

Watts only stared and ejaculated; but Leah, with some colour, for once, in her pale cheeks, clasped her hands. "Oh, sir, I'm thankful you have found it again!" she exclaimed. "I'm heartily thankful!"

"So am I, Leah, though the mystery attending the transaction is as great as ever; indeed, more so."

It certainly was. They went down again, and I sat musing over the problem. But nothing could I make out of it. One moment I argued that the individual taking it (whomsoever it might be) must have had temporary need of funds, and, the difficulty over, had now restored the money. The next, I wondered whether anyone could have taken the bag inadvertently, and had now discovered it. I locked the bag safely up, wrote a letter to George Coney, and then went out to confide the news to Arthur Lake.

Taking the short cuts and passages that lead from Essex Street to the Temple, as I generally did when bound for Lake's chambers, I was passing onwards, when I found myself called to—or I thought so. Standing still in the shade, leaning against the railings of the Temple Gardens, was a slight man of middle height: and he seemed to say "Charley."

Glancing in doubt, half stopping as I did so, yet thinking I must have been mistaken, I was passing on, when the voice came again.

"Charley!"

I stopped then. And I declare that in the revulsion it brought me you might have knocked me down with a feather; for it was Tom Heriot.

"I was almost sure it was you, Charles," he said in a low voice; "but not quite sure."

I had not often had such a scare as this. My heart, with pain and dismay, beat as if it meant to burst its bonds.

"Can it possibly be *you*?" I cried. "What brings you here? Why have you come again?"

"Reached London this morning. Came here when dusk set in, thinking I might have the luck to see you or Lake, Charley."

"But why have you left Scotland? You were safer there."

"Don't know that I was. And I had grown tired to death of it."

"It will end in death, or something like it, if you persist in staying here."

Tom laughed his gay, ringing laugh. I looked round to see that no one was about, or within hearing.

"What a croaker you are, old Charley! I'm sure you ought to kill the fatted calf, to celebrate my return from banishment."

"But, Tom, you *know* how dangerous it is, and must be, for you to be here in London."

"And it was becoming dangerous up there," he quickly rejoined. "Since the summer season set in, those blessed tourists are abroad again, with their staves and knapsacks. No place is safe from them, and the smaller and more obscure it is, the more they are sure to find it. The other day I was in my boat in my fishing toggery, as usual, when a fellow comes up, addresses me as 'My good man,' and plunges into queries touching the sea and the fishing-trade. Now who do you think that was, Charles?"

"I can't say."

"It was James Lawless, Q.C.—the leader who prosecuted at my trial."

"Good heavens!"

"I unfastened the boat, keeping my back to him and my face down, and shot off like a whirlwind, calling out that I was behind time, and must put out. I took good care, Charles, not to get back before the stars were bright in the night sky."

"Did he recognise you?"

"No—no. For certain, no. But he would have done so had I stayed to talk. And it is not always that I could escape as I did then. You must see that."

I saw it all too plainly.

"So I thought it best to make myself scarce, Charles, and leave the tourists' haunts. I sold my boat; no difficulty in that; though, of course, the two men who bought it shaved me; and came over to London as fast as a third-class train would bring me. Dare not put my nose into a first-class carriage, lest I should drop upon some one of my old chums."

"Of all places, Tom, you should not have chosen London."

"Will you tell me, old fellow, what other place I could have pitched upon?"

And I could not tell.

"Go where I will," he continued, "it seems that the Philistines are likely to find me out."

We were pacing about now, side by side, keeping in the shade as much as possible, and speaking under our breath.

"You will have to leave the country, Tom; you must do it. And go somewhere over the seas."

"To Van Diemen's Land, perhaps," suggested Tom.

"Now, be quiet. The subject is too serious for jesting. I should think—perhaps—America. But I must have time to consider. Where do you mean to stay at present? Where are you going to-night?"

"I've been dodging about all day, not showing up much; but I'm going now to where I lodged last, down Blackfriars way. You remember?"

"Yes, I remember: it is not so long ago."

"It is as safe as any other quarter, for aught I can tell. Any way, I don't know of another."

"Are you well, Tom?" I asked. He was looking thin, and seemed to have a nasty cough upon him.

"I caught cold some time ago, and it hangs about me," he replied. "Oh, I shall be all right now I'm here," he added carelessly.

"You ought to take a good jorum of something hot when you get to bed to-night——"

Tom laughed. "I *am* likely to get anything of that sort in any lodging I stand a chance of to-night. Well done, Charley! I haven't old Leah to coddle me."

And somehow the mocking words made me realize the discomforts and deprivations of Tom Heriot's present life. How would it all end?

We parted with a hand-shake: he stealing off on his way to his lodging, I going thoughtfully on mine. It was a calm summer evening, clear and lovely, the stars twinkling in the sky, but all its peace had gone out for me.

It was impossible to foresee what the ending would or could be. At any moment Tom might be recognised and captured, so long as he inhabited London; and it might be difficult to induce him to leave it. Still more difficult to cause him to depart altogether for other lands and climes.

Not long before, I had consulted with Mr. Serjeant Stillingfar as to the possibility of obtaining a pardon for Tom. That he had not been guilty was indisputable, though the law had deemed him so. But the Serjeant had given me no encouragement that any such movement would be successful. The very fact, as he pointed out, of Tom Heriot's having escaped clandestinely, would tell against him. What, I said then, if Tom gave himself up? He smiled, and told me I had better not ask his opinion upon the practical points of the case.

So the old trouble was back again in full force, and I knew not how to cope with it.

The summer sun, glowing with light and heat, lay full upon Hastings and St. Leonard's. The broad expanse of sea sparkled beneath it; the houses that looked on the water were burning and blistering under the fierce rays. Miss Brightman, seated at her drawing-room window, knitting in hand, observed that it was one of the most dazzling days she remembered.

The remark was made to me and to Annabel. We sat at the table together, looking over a book of costly engravings that Miss Brightman had recently bought. "I shall leave it with you, Charles," she said, "when I go away; you will take care of it. And if it were not that you are tied to London, and it would be too far for you to go up and down daily, I would leave you my house also—that you might live in it, and take care of that during my absence."

Mrs. Brightman had come to her senses. Very much, I confess, to my astonishment, much also I think to Annabel's, she had put aside her prejudices and consented to our marriage. The difficulty of where her daughter was to be during Miss Brightman's sojourn in Madeira had in a degree paved the way for it. Annabel would, of course, have returned to her mother; she begged hard to be allowed to do so: she believed it her duty to be with her. But Miss Brightman would not hear of it, and, had she yielded, I should have interposed my veto in Mr. Brightman's name. In Hatch's words, strong in sense but weak in grammar, "their home wasn't no home for Miss Annabel."

Mrs. Brightman could only be conscious of this. During her sojourn at Brighton, and for some little time after her return home, she had been very much better; had fought resolutely with the insidious foe, and conquered. But alas! she fell away again. Now she was almost as bad as ever; tolerably sober by day, very much the opposite by night.

Miss Brightman, dating forward, seeing, as she feared, only shoals and pitfalls, and most anxious for Annabel, had journeyed up to Clapham to her sister-in-law, and stayed there with her a couple of days. What passed between them even Hatch never knew; but she did know that her mistress was brought to a penitent and subdued frame of mind, and that she promised Lucy Brightman, with many tears, to *strive* to overcome her fatal habit for the good God's sake. And it was during this visit that she withdrew her opposition to the marriage; when Miss Brightman returned home she carried the consent with her.

And my present visit to Hastings was to discuss time and place and other matters; more particularly the question of where our home was to be. A large London house we were not yet rich enough to set up, and I would not take Annabel to an inferior one; but I had seen a charming little cottage at Richmond that might suit us—if she liked the locality.

Closing the book of engravings, I turned to Miss Brightman, and entered upon the subject. Suddenly her attention wavered. It seemed to be attracted by something in the road.

"Why, bless my heart, *it is*!" she cried in astonishment. "If ever I saw Hatch in my life, that is Hatch—coming up the street! Annabel, child, give me the glasses."

The glasses were on the table, and I handed them to her. Annabel flew to the window and grew white. She was never free from fears of what might happen in her mother's house. Hatch it was, and apparently in haste.

"What can be the matter?" she gasped. "Oh, Aunt Lucy!"

"Hatch is nodding heartily, as if not much were wrong," remarked Miss Brightman, who was watching her through the glasses. "Hatch is peculiar in manner, as you are aware, Mr. Charles, but she means no disrespect by it."

I smiled. I knew Hatch quite as well as Miss Brightman knew her.

"Now what brings you to Hastings?" she exclaimed, rising from her chair, when Hatch was shown in.

"My missis brought me, ma'am," returned Hatch, with composure. "Miss Annabel, you be looking frighted, but there's nothing wrong. Yesterday morning, all in a flurry like, your mamma took it into her head to come down here, and we drove down with——"

"*Drove* down?"

"Yes, ma'am, with four posters to the carriage. My missis can't abear the rail; she says folks stare at her: and here we be at the Queen's Hotel, she, and me, and Perry."

"Would you like to take a chair, Hatch?" said Miss Brightman.

"My legs is used to standing, ma'am," replied Hatch, with a nod of thanks, "and I've not much time to linger. It was late last night when we got here. This morning, up gets my missis, and downstairs she comes to her breakfast in her sitting-room, and me with her to wait upon her, for sometimes her hands is shaky, and she prefers me to Perry or anybody else——"

"How has your mistress been lately?" interposed Miss Brightman.

"Better, ma'am. Not always quite the thing, though a deal better on the whole. But I must get on about this morning," added Hatch impressively. "'Waiter,' says my missis when the man brings up the coffee. 'Mum?' says he. 'I am subject to spadical attacks in the chest,' says she, 'and should like to have some brandy in my room: they take me sometimes in the middle of the night. Put a bottle into it, the very best French, and a corkscrew. Or you may as well put two bottles,' she goes on; 'I may be here some time.' 'It shall be done, mum,' says he. I was as vexed as I could be to hear it," broke off Hatch, "but what could I do? I couldn't contradict my missis and tell the man that no brandy must be put in her room, or else she'd drink it. Well, ma'am, I goes down presently to my own breakfast with Perry, and while we sat at it a chambermaid comes through the room: 'I've put two bottles of brandy in the lady's bedroom, as was ordered,' says she. With that Perry looks at me all in a fluster—he have no more wits to turn things off than a born idiot. 'Very well,' says I to her, eating at my egg as if I thought nothing; 'I hopes my missis won't have no call to use 'em, but she's took awful bad in the chest sometimes, and it's as well for us to be ready.' 'I'm sure I pities her,' says the girl, 'for there ain't nothing worse than spasms. I has 'em myself occasional——'"

When once Hatch was in the full flow of a narrative, there was no getting in a word edgeways, and Miss Brightman had to repeat her question twice: "Does Perry know the nature of the illness that affects Mrs. Brightman?"

"Why, in course he does, ma'am," was Hatch's rejoinder. "He couldn't be off guessing it for himself, and the rest I told him. Why, ma'am, without his helping, we could never keep it dark from the servants at home. It was better to make a confidant of Perry, that I might have his aid in screening the trouble, than to let it get round to everybody. He's as safe and sure as I be, and when it all first came out to him, he cried over it, to think of what his poor master must have suffered in mind before death took him. Well, ma'am, I made haste over my breakfast, and I went upstairs, and there was the bottles and the corkscrew, so I whips 'em off the table and puts them out of sight. Mrs. Brightman comes up presently, and looks about and goes down again. Three separate times she comes up, and the third time she gives the bell a whirl, and in runs the chambermaid, who was only outside. 'I gave orders this morning,' says my lady, 'to have some brandy placed in the room.' 'Oh, I have got the brandy,' says I, before the girl could speak; 'I put it in the little cupboard here, ma'am.' So away goes the girl, looking from the corners of her eyes at me, as if suspicious I meant to crib it for my own use: and my mistress began: 'Draw one of them corks, Hatch.' 'No, ma'am,' says I, 'not yet; please don't.' 'Draw 'em both,' says missis—for there are times," added Hatch, "when a trifle puts her out so much that it's hazardous to cross her. I drew the cork of one, and missis just pointed with her finger to the tumbler on the wash-handstand, and I brought it forward and the decanter of water. 'Now you may go,' says she; so I took up the corkscrew. 'I told you to leave that,' says she, in her temper, and I had to come away without it, and the minute I was gone she turned the key upon me. Miss Annabel, I see the words are grieving of you, but they are the truth, and I can but tell them."

"Is she there now—locked in?" asked Miss Brightman.

"She's there now," returned Hatch, with solemn enunciation, to make up for her failings in grammar, which was never anywhere in times of excitement; "she is locked in with them two bottles and the corkscrew, and she'll just drink herself mad—and what's to be done? I goes at once to Perry and tells him. 'Let's get in through the winder,' says Perry—which his brains is only fit for a gander, as I've said many a time. 'You stop outside her door to listen again downright harm,' says I, 'that's what you'll do; and I'll go for Miss Brightman.' And here I'm come, ma'am, running all the way."

"What can I do?" wailed Miss Brightman.

"Ma'am," answered Hatch, "I think that if you'll go back with me, and knock at her room door, and call out that you be come to pay her a visit, she'd undo it. She's more afeared of you than of anybody living. She can't have done herself much harm yet, and you might coax her out for a walk or a drive, and then bring her in to dinner here—anything to get her away from them two dangerous bottles. If I be making too free, ma'am, you'll be good enough to excuse me—it is for the family's sake. At home I can manage her pretty well, but to have a scene at the hotel would make it public."

"What is to be the ending?" I exclaimed involuntarily as Miss Brightman went in haste for her bonnet.

"Why, the ending must be—just what it will be," observed Hatch philosophically. "But, Mr. Charles, I don't despair of her yet. Begging your pardon, Miss Annabel, you'd better not come. Your mamma won't undo her door if she thinks there's many round it."

Annabel stood at the window as they departed, her face turned from me, her eyes blinded with tears. I drew her away, though I hardly knew how to soothe her. It was a heavy grief to bear.

"My days are passed in dread of what tidings may be on the way to me," she began, after a little time given to gathering composure. "I ought to be nearer my mother, Charles; I tell Aunt Lucy so almost every day. She might be ill and dead before I could get to her, up in London."

"And you will be nearer to her shortly, Annabel. My dear, where shall our home be? I was thinking of Richmond——"

"No, no," she interrupted in sufficient haste to show me she had thoughts of her own.

"Annabel! It shall not be *there*: at your mother's. Anywhere else."

"It is somewhere else that I want to be."

"Then you shall be. Where is it?"

She lifted her face like a pleading child's, and spoke in a whisper. "Charles, let me come to you in Essex Street."

"*Essex Street!*" I echoed in surprise. "My dear Annabel, I will certainly not bring you to Essex Street and its inconveniences. I cannot do great things for you yet, but I can do better than that."

"They would not be inconveniences to me. I would turn them into pleasures. We would take another servant to help Watts and Leah; or two if necessary. You would not find me the least encumbrance; I would never be in the way of your professional rooms. And in the evening, when you had finished for the day, we would dine, and go down to mamma's for an hour, and then back again. Charles, it would be a happy home: let me come to it."

But I shook my head. I did not see how it could be arranged; and said so.

"No, because at present the idea is new to you," returned Annabel. "*Think it over*, Charles. Promise me that you will do so."

"Yes, my dear; I can at least promise you that."

There was less trouble with Mrs. Brightman that day than had been anticipated. She opened her door at once to her sister-in-law, who brought her back to the Terrace. Hatch had been wise. In the afternoon we all went for a drive in a fly, and returned to dinner. And the following day Mrs. Brightman, with her servants, departed for London in her travelling-carriage, no scandal whatever having been caused at the Queen's Hotel. I went up by train early in the morning.

It is surprising how much thinking upon a problem simplifies it. I began to see by degrees that Annabel's coming to Essex Street could be easily managed; nay, that it would be for the best. Miss Brightman strongly advocated it. At present a large portion of my income had to be paid over to Mrs. Brightman in accordance with her husband's will, so that I could not do as I would, and must study economy. Annabel would be rich in time; for Mrs. Brightman's large income, vested at present in trustees, must eventually descend to Annabel; but that time was not yet. And who knew what expenses Tom Heriot might bring upon me?

Changes had to be made in the house. I determined to confine the business rooms to the ground floor; making Miss Methold's parlour, which had not been much used since her death, my own private consulting-room. The front room on the first floor would be our drawing-room, the one behind it the dining-room.

Leah was in an ecstasy when she heard the news. The workmen were coming in to paint and paper, and then I told her.

"Of course, Mr. Charles, it—is——"

"Is what, Leah?"

"Miss Annabel."

"It should be no one else, Leah. We shall want another servant or two, but you can still be major-domo."

"If my poor master had only lived to see it!" she uttered, with enthusiasm. "How happy he would have been; how proud to have her here! Well, well, what turns things take!"

CHAPTER V.
CONFESSION.

OCTOBER came in; and we were married early in the month, the wedding taking place from Mrs. Brightman's residence, as was of course only right and proper. It was so very quiet a wedding that there is not the least necessity for describing it—and how can a young man be expected to give the particulars of his own? Mr. Serjeant Stillingfar was present; Lord and Lady Level, now staying in London, drove down for it; and Captain Chantrey gave his niece away. For Mrs. Brightman had chosen to request him to accept her invitation to do so, and to be accompanied by his wife, Lady Grace. Miss Brightman was also present, having travelled up from Hastings the day before. Three or four days later on, she would sail for Madeira.

I could not spare more than a fortnight from work, leaving Lennard as my locum tenens. Annabel would have been glad to spare less, for she was haunted by visions of what might happen to her mother. Though there was no especial cause for anxiety in that quarter just now, she could never feel at ease. And on my part I was more anxious than ever about Tom Heriot, for more reasons than one.

The fortnight came to an end, all too soon: and late on the Saturday evening we reached home. Watts threw open the door, and there stood Leah in a silk gown. The drawing-room, gayer than it used to be, was bright with a fire and preparations for tea.

"How homelike it looks!" exclaimed Annabel. "Charles," she whispered, turning to me with her earnest eyes, as she had been wont to do when a child: "I will not make the least noise when you have clients with you. You shall not know I am in the house: I will take care not to drop even a reel of cotton on the carpet. I do thank you for letting me come to Essex Street: I should not have seemed so completely your wife had you taken me to any but your old home."

The floors above were also in order, their chambers refurnished. Leah went up to them with her new mistress, and I went down to the clerks' office, telling Annabel I should not be there five minutes. One of the clerks, Allen, had waited; but I had expected Lennard.

"Is Mr. Lennard not here?" I asked. "Did he not wait? I wrote to him to do so."

"Mr. Lennard has not been here all day, sir," was Allen's reply. "A messenger came from him this morning, to say he was ill."

We were deep in letters and other matters, I and Allen, when the front door opened next the office door, and there stood Arthur Lake, laughing, a light coat on his arm.

"Fancy! I've been down the river for a blow," cried he. "Just landed at the pier here. Seeing lights in your windows, I thought you must have got back, Charley."

We shook hands, and he stayed a minute, talking. Then, wishing good-night to Allen, he backed out of the room, making an almost imperceptible movement to me with his head. I followed him out, shutting the office door behind me. Lake touched my arm and drew me outside.

"I suppose you've not heard from Tom Heriot since you were away," breathed Lake, in cautious tones, as we stood together on the outer step.

"No; I did not expect to hear. Why?"

"I saw him three days ago," whispered Lake. "I had a queer-looking letter on Wednesday morning from one Mr. Dominic Turk, asking me to call at a certain place in Southwark. Of course, I guessed it was Tom, and that he had moved his lodgings again; and I found I was right."

"Dominic Turk!" I repeated. "Does he call himself *that*?"

Lake laughed. "He is passing now for a retired schoolmaster. Says he's sure nobody can doubt he is one as long as he sticks to that name."

"How is he? Has any fresh trouble turned up? I'm sure you've something bad to tell me."

"Well, Charley, honestly speaking, it is a bad look-out, in more ways than one," he answered. "He is very ill, to begin with; also has an idea that a certain policeman named Wren has picked up an inkling of his return, and is trying to unearth him. But," added Lake, "we can't very well talk in this place. I've more to say———"

"Come upstairs, and take tea with me and Annabel," I interrupted.

"Can't," said he; "my dinner's waiting. I'm back two hours later than I expected to be; it has been frizzling, I expect, all the time. Besides, old fellow, I'd rather you and I were alone. There's fearful peril looming ahead, unless I'm mistaken. Can you come round to my chambers to-morrow afternoon?"

"No: we are going to Mrs. Brightman's after morning service."

"It must be left until Monday, then; but I don't think there's much time to be lost. Good-night."

Lake hastened up the street, and I returned to Allen and the letters.

With this interruption, and with all I found to do, the five minutes' absence I had promised my wife lengthened into twenty. At last the office was closed for the night, Allen left, and I ran upstairs, expecting to have kept Annabel waiting tea. She was not in the drawing-room, the tea was not made, and I went up higher and found her sobbing in the bedroom. It sent me into a cold chill.

"My love, what is this? Are you disappointed? Are you not happy?"

"Oh, Charles," she sobbed, clinging to me, "you *know* I am happy. It is not that. But I could not help thinking of my father. Leah got talking about him; and I remembered once his sitting in that very chair, holding me on his knee. I must have been about seven years old. Miss Methold was ill——"

At that moment there came a knock and a ring at the front door. Not a common knock and ring, but sharp, loud and prolonged, resounding through the house as from some impatient messenger of evil. It startled us both. Annabel's fears flew to her mother; mine to a different quarter, for Lake's communication was troubling and tormenting me.

"Charles! if——"

"Hush, dear. Listen."

As we stood outside on the landing, her heart beating against my encircling hand, and our senses strained to listen, we heard Watts open the front door.

"Has Mr. Strange come home?" cried a voice hurriedly—that of a woman.

"Yes," said Watts.

"Can I speak to him? It is on a matter of life and death."

"Where do you come from?" asked Watts, with habitual caution.

"I come from Mr. Lennard. Oh, pray do not waste time!"

"All right, my darling; it is not from your mother," I whispered to Annabel, as I ran down.

A young woman stood at the foot of the stairs; I was at a loss to guess her condition in life. She had the face and manner of a lady, but her dress was poor and shabby.

"I have come from my father, sir—Mr. Lennard," she said in a low tone, blushing very much. "He is dangerously ill: we fear he is dying, and so does he. He bade me say that he must see you, or he cannot die in peace. Will you please be at the trouble of coming?"

One hasty word despatched to my wife, and I went out with Miss Lennard, hailing a cab, which had just set down its freight some doors higher up. "What is the matter with your father?" I questioned, as we whirled along towards Blackfriars Bridge, in accordance with her directions.

"It is an attack of inward inflammation," she replied. "He was taken ill suddenly last night after he got home from the office, and he has been in great agony all day. This evening he grew better; the pain almost subsided; but the doctor said that might not prove a favourable symptom. My father asked for the truth—whether he was dying, and the answer was that he might be. Then my father grew terribly uneasy in mind, and said he must see you if possible before he died—and sent me to ascertain, sir, whether you had returned home."

The cab drew up at a house in a side street, a little beyond Blackfriars Bridge. We entered, and Miss Lennard left me in the front sitting-room. The remnants of faded gentility were strangely mixed with bareness and poverty. Poor Lennard was a gentleman born and bred, but had been reduced by untoward misfortune. Trifling ornaments stood about; "antimacassars" were thrown over the shabby chairs. Miss Lennard had gone upstairs, but came down quickly.

"It is the door on the left, sir, on the second landing," said she, putting a candle in my hand. "My father is anxiously expecting you, but says I am not to go up."

It was a small landing, nothing in front of me but a bare white-washed wall, and *two* doors to the left. I blundered into the wrong one. A night-cap border turned on the bed, and a girlish face looked up from under it.

"What do you want?" she said.

"Pardon me. I am in search of Mr. Lennard."

"Oh, it is the next room. But—sir! wait a moment. Oh, wait, wait!"

I turned to her in surprise, and she put up two thin white hands in an imploring attitude. "Is it anything bad? Have you come to take him?"

"To take him! What do you mean?"

"You are not a sheriff's officer?"

I smiled at her troubled countenance. "I am Mr. Strange—come to see how he is."

Down fell her hands peacefully. "Sir, I beg your pardon: thank you for telling me. I know papa has sometimes been in apprehension, and I lie here and fear things till I am stupid. A strange step on the stairs, or a strange knock at the door, sets me shaking."

The next room was the right one, and Lennard was lying in it on a low bed; his face looked ghastly, his eyes wildly anxious.

"Lennard," I said, "I am sorry to hear of your illness. What's the matter?"

"Sit down, Mr. Strange; sit down," he added, pointing to a chair, which I drew near. "It is an attack of inflammation: the pain has ceased now, but the doctor says it is an uncertain symptom: it may be for better, or it may be for worse. If the latter, I have not many hours to live."

"What brought it on?"

"I don't know: unless it was that I drank a draught of cold water when I was hot. I have not been very strong for some time, and a little thing sends me into a violent heat. I had a long walk, four miles, and I made nearly a run of it half the way, being pressed for time. When I got in, I asked Leah for some water, and drank two glasses of it, one after the other. It seemed to strike a chill to me at the time."

"It was at the office, then. Four miles! Why did you not ride?"

"It was not your business I was out on, sir; it was my own. But whether that was the cause or not, the illness came on, and it cannot be remedied now. If I am to die, I must die; God is over all: but I cannot go without making a confession to you. How the fear of death's approach alters a man's views and feelings!" he went on, in a different tone. "Yesterday, had I been told I must make this confession to you, I should have said, Let me die, rather; but it appears to me now to be an imperative duty, and one I must nerve myself to perform."

Lennard lay on his pillow, and looked fixedly at me, and I not less fixedly at him. What, in the shape of a "confession," could he have to make to me? He had been managing clerk in Mr. Brightman's office long before I was in it, a man of severe integrity, and respected by all.

"The night Mr. Brightman died," he began under his panting breath, "the bag of gold was missing—George Coney's. You remember it."

"Well?"

"I took it."

Was Lennard's mind wandering? He was no more likely to take gold than I was. I sat still, gazing at him.

"Yes, it was I who took it, sir. Will you hear the tale?"

A deep breath, and the drawing of my chair closer to his bedside, was my only answer.

"You are a young man, Mr. Strange. I have taken an interest in you since you first came, a lad, into the office, and were under my authority—Charles, do this; Charles, do the other. Not that I have shown any especial interest, for outwardly I am cold and undemonstrative; but I saw what you were, and liked you in my heart. You are a young man yet, I say; but, liking you, hoping for your welfare, I pray Heaven that it may never be your fate, in after-life, to be trammelled with misfortunes as I have been. For me they seem to have had no end, and the worst of them in later years has been that brought upon me by an undutiful and spendthrift son."

In a moment there flashed into my mind *my* later trouble in Tom Heriot: I seemed to be comparing the one with the other. "Have you been trammelled with an undutiful son?" I said aloud.

"I have been, and am," replied Lennard. "It has been my later cross. The first was that of losing my property and position in life, for, as you know, Mr. Strange, I was born and reared a gentleman. The last cross has been Leonard—that is his name, Leonard Lennard—and it has been worse than the first, for it has kept us *down*, and in a perpetual ferment for years. It has kept us poor amongst the poor: my salary, as you know, is a handsome one, but it has chiefly to be wasted upon him."

"What age is he?"

"Six-and-twenty yesterday."

"Then you are not forced to supply his extravagance, to find money for his faults and follies. You are not obliged to let him keep you down."

"By law, no," sighed poor Lennard. "But these ill-doing sons sometimes entwine themselves around your very heartstrings; far rather would you suffer and suffer than not ward off the ill from them. He has tried his hand at many occupations, but remains at none; the result is always trouble: and yet his education and intellect, his good looks and perfect, pleasant manners, would fit him for almost any responsible position in life. But he is reckless. Get into what scrape he would, whether of debt, or worse, here he was sure of a refuge and a welcome; I received him, his mother and sisters loved him. One of them is bedridden," he added, in an altered tone.

"I went first by mistake into the next room. I probably saw her."

"Yes, that's Maria. It is a weakness that has settled in her legs; some chronic affection, I suppose; and there she has lain for ten months. With medical attendance and sea air she might be restored, they tell me, but I can provide neither. Leonard's claims have been too heavy."

"But should you waste means on him that ought to be applied to her necessities?" I involuntarily interrupted.

He half raised himself on his elbow, and the effort proved how weak he was, and his eyes and his voice betrayed a strange earnestness. "When a son, whom you love better than life itself, has to be saved from the consequences of his follies, from prison, from worse disgrace even than that, other interests are forgotten, let them be what they may. Silent, patient needs give way to obtrusive wants that stare you in the face, and that may bear fear and danger in their train. Mr. Strange, you can imagine this."

"I do. It must ever be so."

"The pecuniary wants of a young man, such as my son is, are as the cry of the horse-leech. Give! give! Leonard mixes sometimes with distant relatives, young fellows of fashion, who are moving in a sphere far above our present position, although I constantly warn him not to do it. One of these wants, imperative and to be provided for in some way or other, occurred the beginning of February in this year. How I managed to pay it I can hardly tell, but it stripped me of all the money I could raise, and left me with some urgent debts upon me. The rent was owing, twelve months the previous December, and some of the tradespeople were becoming clamorous. The landlord, discerning the state of affairs, put in a distress, terrifying poor Maria, whose illness had then not very long set in, almost to death. That I had the means to pay the man out you may judge, when I tell you that we had not the money to buy a joint of meat or a loaf of bread."

Lennard paused to wipe the dew from his brow.

"Maria was in bed, wanting comforts; Charlotte was worn out with apprehension; Leonard was away again, and we had nothing. Of my wife I will not speak: of delicate frame and delicately reared, the long-continued troubles have reduced her to a sort of dumb apathy. No credit anywhere, and a distress in for rent! In sheer despair, I resolved to disclose part of my difficulty to Mr. Brightman, and ask him to advance me a portion of my next quarter's salary. I hated to do it. A reduced gentleman is, perhaps, over-fastidious. I know I have been so, and my pride rose against it. In health, I could not have spoken to you, Mr. Charles, as I am now doing. I went on, shilly-shallying for a few days. On the Saturday morning Charlotte came to me with a whisper: 'That man in the house says if the rent is not paid to-night, the things will be taken out and sold on Monday: it is the very last day they'll give.' I went to the office, my mind made up at length, and thinking what I should say to Mr. Brightman. Should I tell him part of the truth, or should I urge some plea, foreign to it? It was an unusually busy day: I dare say you remember it, Mr. Charles, for it was that of Mr. Brightman's sudden death. Client after client called, and no opportunity offered for my speaking to him in private. I waited for him to come down, on his way out in the evening, thinking I would speak to him then. He did not come, and when the clients left, and I went upstairs, I found he was stopping in town to see Sir Edmund Clavering. I should have spoken to him then, but you were present. He told me to look in again in the course of the evening, and I hoped I might find him alone then. You recollect the subsequent events of the night, sir?"

"I shall never forget them."

"When I came in, as he directed me, between seven and eight o'clock, there occurred that flurry with Leah—the cause of which I never knew. She said Mr. Brightman was alone, and I went up. He was lying in your room, Mr. Charles; had fallen close to his own desk, the deep drawer of which stood open. I tried to raise him; I sprinkled water on his face, but I saw that he was dead. On the desk lay a small canvas bag. I took it up and shook it. Why, I do not know, for I declare that no wrong thought had then come into my mind. He appeared to have momentarily put it out of the drawer, probably in search of something, for his private cheque-book and the key of the iron safe, that I knew were always kept in the drawer, lay near it. I shook the bag, and its contents sounded like gold. I opened it, and counted thirty sovereigns. Mr. Brightman was dead. I could not apply to him; and yet money I must have. The temptation upon me was strong, and I took it. Don't turn away from me, sir. There are some temptations too strong to be resisted by a man in his necessities."

"Indeed, I am not turning from you. The temptation was overwhelmingly great."

"Indeed," continued the sick man, "the devil was near me then. I put the key and the cheque-book inside, and I locked the drawer, and placed the keys in Mr. Brightman's pocket, where he kept them, and I leaped down the stairs with the bag in my hand. It was all done in a minute or two of time, though it seems long in relating it. Where should I put the bag, now I had it? Upon my person? No: it might be missed directly, and inquired for. I was in a tumult—scarcely sane, I believe—and I dashed into the clerks' office, and, taking off the lid of the coal-box, put it there. Then I tore off for a surgeon. You know the rest. When I returned with him you were there; and the next visitor, while we were standing round Mr. Brightman, was George Coney, after his bag of money. I never shall forget the feeling when you motioned me to take Mr. Brightman's keys from his pocket to get the bag out of the drawer. Or when—after it was missed—you took me with you to search for it, in the very office where it was, and I moved the coal-box under the desk. Had you only happened to lift the lid, sir!"

"Ah!"

"When the search was over, and I went home, I had put the bag in my breastpocket. The gold saved me from immediate trouble, but——"

"You have sent it back to me, you know—the bag and the thirty pounds."

"Yes, I sent it back—tardily. I *could* not do it earlier, though the crime coloured my days with remorse, and I never knew a happy moment until it was restored. But Leonard had been back again, and restoration was not easy."

Miss Lennard opened the door at this juncture. "Papa, the doctor is here. Can he come up? He says he ought to see you."

"Oh, certainly, he must come up," I interposed.

"Yes, yes, Charlotte," said Lennard.

The doctor came in, and stood looking at his patient, after putting a few questions. "Well," said he, "you are better; you will get over it."

"Do you really think so?" I asked joyfully.

"Decidedly I do, now. It has been a sharp twinge, but the danger's over. You see, when pain suddenly ceases, mortification sometimes sets in, and I could not be sure. But you will do this time, Mr. Lennard."

Lennard had little more to say; and, soon after the doctor left, I prepared to follow him.

"There's a trifle of salary due to me, Mr. Strange," he whispered; "that which has been going on since Quarter Day. I suppose you will not keep it from me?"

"Keep it from you! No. Why should I? Do you want it at once? You can have it if you do."

Leonard looked up wistfully. "You do not think of taking me back again? You will not do that?"

"Yes, I will. You and I shall understand each other better than ever now."

The tears welled up to his eyes. He laid his other hand—I had taken one—across his face. I bent over him with a whisper.

"What has passed to-night need never be recurred to between us; and I shall never speak of it to another. We all have our trials and troubles, Lennard. A very weighty one is lying now upon me, though it is not absolutely my own—*brought* upon me, you see, as yours was. And it is worse than yours."

"Worse!" he exclaimed, looking at me.

"More dangerous in its possible consequences. Now mind," I broke off, shaking him by the hand, "you are not to attempt to come to Essex Street until you are quite strong enough for it. But I shall see you here again on Monday, for I have two or three questions to ask you as to some of the matters that have transpired during my absence. Good-night, Lennard; keep up a good heart; you will outlive your trials yet."

And when I left him he was fairly sobbing.

CHAPTER VI.
DANGER.

MRS. BRIGHTMAN was certainly improving. When I reached her house with Annabel on the following day, Sunday, between one and two o'clock, she was bright and cheerful, and came towards the entrance-gates to meet us. She, moreover, displayed interest in all we told her of our honeymoon in the Isle of Wight, and of the places we had visited. Besides that, I noticed that she took water with her dinner.

"If she'll only keep to it," said Hatch, joining me in her unceremonious fashion as I strolled in the garden later, smoking a cigar. "Yes, Mr. Charles, she's trying hard to put bad habits away from her, and I hope she'll be able to do it."

"I hope and trust she will!"

"Miss Brightman went back to Hastings the day after the wedding-day," continued Hatch; "but before she started she had a long interview with my mistress, they two shut up in missis's bedroom alone. For pretty nigh all the rest of the day, my missis was in tears, and she has not touched nothing strong since."

"Nothing at all!" I cried in surprise, for it seemed too good to be true. "Why, that's a fortnight ago! More than a fortnight."

"Well, it is so, Mr. Charles. Not but that missis has tried as long and as hard before now—and failed again."

It was Monday evening before I could find time to go round to Lake's—and he did not come to me. He was at home, poring over some difficult law case by lamp-light.

"Been in court all day, Charley," he cried. "Have not had a minute to spare for you."

"About Tom?" I said, as I sat down. "You seemed to say that you had more unpleasantness to tell me."

"Aye, about Tom," he replied, turning his chair to face me, and propping his right elbow upon his table. "Well, I fear Tom is in a bad way."

"In health, you mean?"

"I do. His cough is frightful, and he is more like a skeleton than a living being. I should say the illness has laid hold of his lungs."

"Has he had a doctor?"

"No. Asks how he is to have one. Says a doctor might (they were his own words) smell a rat. Doctors are not called in to the class of people lodging in that house unless they are dying: and it would soon be seen by any educated man that Tom is not of *their* kind. My opinion is, that a doctor could not do him much good now," added Lake.

He looked at me as he spoke; to see, I suppose, whether I took in his full meaning. I did—unhappily.

"And what do you think he is talking of now, Charles?" returned Lake. "Of giving himself up."

"Giving himself up! What, to justice?"

Lake nodded. "You know what Tom Heriot is—not much like other people."

"But why should he think of *that*? It would end everything."

"I was on the point of asking him why," said Lake. "Whether I should have had a satisfactory answer, I cannot say; I should think he could not give one; but we were interrupted. Miss Betsy Lee came in."

"Who? What?" I cried, starting from my chair.

"The young lady you told me of who lives in Lambeth—Miss Betsy Lee. Sit down, Charley. She came over to bring him a pot of jelly."

"Then he has let those people know where he is, Lake! Is he mad?"

"Mad as to carelessness," assented Lake. "I tell you Tom Heriot's not like other people."

"He will leave himself no chance."

"She seems to be a nice, modest little woman," said Lake; "and I'll go bail her visit was quite honest and proper. She had made this jelly, she told Tom, and she and her father hoped it would serve to strengthen him, and her father sent his respects, and hopes to hear that Captain Strange was feeling better."

"Well, Lake, the matter will get beyond me," I said in despair. "Only a word dropped, innocently, by these people in some dangerous quarter, and where will Tom be?"

"That's just it," said Lake. "Policeman Wren is acquainted with them."

"Did you leave the girl there?"

"No. Some rough man came into the room smoking, and sat down, evidently with the intention of making an evening of it; he lives in the same house and has made acquaintance with Tom, or Tom with him. So I said good-night, and the girl did the same, and we went down together. 'Don't you think Captain Strange looks very ill, sir?' said she as we got into the street. 'I'm afraid he does,' I answered. 'I'm sure he does, sir,' she said. 'It's a woeful pity that somebody should be coming upon him for a big back debt just now, obliging him to keep quiet in a low quarter!' So that is what Tom has told his Lambeth friends," concluded Lake.

Lake gave me the address in Southwark, and I determined to see Tom the next evening. In that, however, I was disappointed. One of our oldest clients, passing through London from the country on his way to Pau, summoned me to him on the Tuesday evening.

But I went on Wednesday. The stars were shining overhead as I traversed the silent street, making out Tom's lodgings. He had only an attic bedroom, I found, and I went up to it. He was partly lying across the bed when I entered.

I almost thought even then that I saw death written in his face. White, wan, shadowy it looked; much changed, much worn from what it was three weeks before. But it lighted up with a smile, as he got up to greet me.

"Halloa, Charley!" cried he. "Best congratulations! Made yourself into a respectable man. All good luck to yourself and madam. I'm thinking of coming to Essex Street to pay the wedding visit."

"Thank you," said I, "but do be serious. My coming here is a hazard, as you know, Tom; don't let us waste in nonsense the few minutes I may stay."

"Nonsense!" cried Tom. "Why, do you think I should be afraid to venture to Essex Street?—what nonsense is there in that? Look here, Charley!"

From some box in a dark corner of the room, he got out an old big blue cloak lined with red, and swung it on. The collar, made of some black curly wool, stood up above his ears. He walked about the small room, exhibiting himself.

"Would the sharpest officer in Scotland Yard take me for anyone but old Major Carlen?" laughed he. "I'm sure I look like his double in this elegant cloak. It was his, once."

"His! What, Major Carlen's?"

"Just so. He made me a present of it."

"You have seen him, then!"

"I sent for him," answered Tom, putting off the old cloak and coughing painfully after his recent exertion. "I thought I should like to see the old fellow; I was not afraid he'd betray me; Carlen would not do that; and I dropped a quiet note to his club, taking the chance of his being in town."

"Taking the chance! Suppose he had not been in town, Tom, and the note had fallen into wrong hands—some inquisitive waiter, let us say, who chose to open it?"

"Well—what then? A waiter would only turn up his nose at Mr. Dominic Turk, the retired schoolmaster, and close up the note again for the Major."

"And what would Major Carlen make of Mr. Dominic Turk?"

"Major Carlen would know my handwriting, Charley."

"And he came in answer to it?"

"He came: and blew me up in a loud and awful fashion; seemed to be trying to blow the ceiling off. First, he threatened to go out and bring in the police; next, he vowed he would go straight to Blanche and tell her all. Finally, he calmed down and promised to send me one of his cast-off cloaks to disguise me, in case I had to go into the streets. Isn't it a beauty?"

"Well, now, Tom, if you can be serious for once, what is going to become of you, and what is to be done? I've come to know."

"Wish I could tell you; don't know myself," said he lightly.

"What was it you said to Lake about giving yourself up?"

"Upon my word of honour, Charley, I sometimes feel inclined to do it. I couldn't be much worse off in prison than I am here. Sick and sad, lad, needing comforts that can't be had in such a place as this; no one to see after me, no one to attend to me. Anyway, it would end the suspense."

I sat turning things about in my mind. It all seemed so full of hazard. That he must be got away from his present quarters was certain. I told him so.

"But you are so recklessly imprudent, you see, Tom," I observed, "and it increases the risk. You have had Miss Betsy Lee here."

Tom flung himself back with a laugh. "She has been here twice, the good little soul. The old man came once."

"Don't you think you might as well take up your standing to-morrow on the top of the Monument, and proclaim yourself to the public at large? You try me greatly, Tom!"

"Try you because I see the Lees! Come, Charley, that's good. They are as safe as you are."

"In intention perhaps. How came you to let them know you were to be found here?"

"How came I?" he carelessly rejoined. "Let's see? Oh, I remember. One evening when I was hipped, fit to die of it all and of the confinement to this wretched room, I strolled out. My feet took me to the old ground—Lambeth—and to Lee's. He chanced to see me, and invited me in. Over some whisky and water, I opened out my woes to them; not of course the truth, but as near as might be. Told them of a curmudgeon creditor of past days that I feared was coming down upon me, so that I had to be in close hiding for a bit."

"But you need not have told them where."

"Oh, they'll be cautious. Miss Betsy was so much struck with my cough and my looks that she said she should make some jelly for me, of the kind she used to make for her mother before she died; and the good little girl has brought me some over here twice in a jar. They are all right, Charley."

It was of no use contending with him. After sitting a little time longer, I promised that he should shortly see me again or hear from me, and took my departure. Full of doubt and trouble, I wanted to be alone, to decide, if possible, what was to be done.

What to do about Tom I knew not. That he required nursing and nourishment, and that he ought to be moved where he could have it, was indisputable. But—the risk!

Three-parts of the night I lay awake, thinking of different plans. None seemed feasible. In the morning I was hardly fit for my day's work, and set to it with unsteady nerves and a worried brain. If I had only someone to consult with, some capable man who would help me! I did think of Mr. Serjeant Stillingfar; but I knew he would not like it, would probably refuse advice. One who now and again sat in the position of judge, sentencing men himself, would scarcely choose to aid in concealing an escaped convict.

I was upstairs in the dining-room at one o'clock, taking luncheon with Annabel, when the door was thrown back by Watts and there loomed into the room the old blue cloak with the red lining. For a moment I thought it was the one I had seen the past night in Southwark, and my heart leaped into my mouth. Watts's quiet announcement dispelled the alarm.

"Major Carlen, sir."

The Major unclasped his cloak after shaking hands with us, and flung it across the sofa, just as Tom had flung his on the bed. I pointed to the cold beef, and asked if he would take some.

"Don't mind if I do, Charles," said he, drawing a chair to the table: "I'm too much bothered just now to eat as I ought. A pretty kettle of fish this is, lad, that you and I have had brought upon us!"

I gave him a warning look, glancing at Annabel. The old fellow understood me—she had not been trusted with the present trouble. That Tom Heriot had effected his escape, Annabel knew; that it was expected he would make his way home, she knew; but that he had long been here, and was now close at hand, I had never told her. Why inflict upon her the suspense I had to endure?

"Rather a chilly day for the time of year," observed the Major, as he coughed down his previous words. "Just a little, Mrs. Strange; underdone, please."

Annabel, who carved at luncheon-time, helped him carefully. "And what kettle of fish is it that you and Charles are troubled with, Major?" she inquired, smiling.

"Ah—aw—don't care to say much about it," answered the Major, more ready at an excuse than I should have deemed him. "Blanche is up to her ears in anger against Level; says she'll get a separation from him, and all that kind of nonsense. But you and I may as well not make it our business, Charles, I expect: better let married folk fight out their own battles. And have you heard from your Aunt Lucy yet, Mrs. Strange?"

So the subject was turned off for the time; but down below, in my office, the Major went at it tooth and nail, talking himself into a fever. All the hard names in the Major's vocabulary were hurled at Tom. His original sin was disgraceful enough, never to be condoned, said the Major; but his present imprudent procedure was worse, and desperately wicked.

"Are Blanche and her husband still at variance?" I asked, when he had somewhat cooled down on the other subject.

"They just are, and are likely to remain so," growled the Major. "It's Blanche's fault. Men have ways of their own, and she's a little fool for wishing to interfere with his. Don't let your wife begin that, Charles; it's my best advice to you. You are laughing, young fellow! Well, perhaps you and Level don't row in quite the same boat; but you can't foresee the shoals you may pitch into. No one can."

We were interrupted by Lennard, who had come back on the previous day, pale and pulled down by his sharp attack of illness, but the same efficient man of business as ever. A telegram had been delivered, which he could not deal with without me.

"I'll be off, then," said the Major; "I suppose I'm only hindering work. And I wish you well through your difficulties, Charles," he added significantly. "I wish all of us well through them. Good-day, Mr. Lennard."

The Major was ready enough to wish *that*, but he could not suggest any means by which it might be accomplished. I had asked him; and he confessed himself incompetent to advise. "I should send him off to sea in a whaling-boat and keep him there," was all the help he gave.

Lennard stayed beyond time that evening, and was ready in my private room to go over certain business with me that had transpired during my own absence. I could not give the necessary attention to it, try as earnestly as I would: Tom and *his* business kept dancing in my brain to the exclusion of other things. Lennard asked me whether I was ill.

"No," I answered; "at least, not in body." And as I spoke, the thought crossed me to confide the trouble to Lennard. He had seen too much trouble himself not to be safe and cautious, and perhaps he might suggest something.

"Let Captain Heriot come to me," he immediately said. "He could not be safer anywhere. Sometimes we let our drawing-room floor; it is vacant now, and he can have it. My wife and my daughter Charlotte will attend to his comforts and nurse him, if that may be, into health. It is the best thing that can be done with him, Mr. Charles."

I saw that it was, seeming to discern all the advantages of the proposal at a grasp, and accepted it. We consulted as to how best to effect Tom's removal, which Lennard himself undertook. I dropped a hasty note to "Mr. Turk" to prepare him to be in readiness the following evening, and Lennard posted it when he went out. He had no sooner gone, than the door of my private room slowly opened, and, rather to my surprise, Leah appeared.

"I beg your pardon, sir, for presuming to disturb you here," she said; "but I can't rest. There's some great trouble afloat; I've seen it in your looks and ways, sir, ever since Sunday. Your face couldn't deceive me when you were my little nursling, Master Charles, and it can't deceive me now. Is it about Mr. Tom?"

"Well, yes, it is, Leah."

Her face turned white. "He has not got himself taken, surely!"

"No; it's not so bad as that—yet."

"Thank Heaven for it!" she returned. "I knew it was him, and I'm all in a twitter about him from morning till night. I can't sleep or eat for dreading the news that any moment may bring of him. It seems to me, Mr. Charles, that one must needs be for ever in a twitter in this world; before one trouble is mended, another turns up. No sooner am I a bit relieved about poor Nancy, that unfortunate daughter of mine, than there comes Mr. Tom."

The relief that Leah spoke of was this: some relatives of Leah's former husband, Nancy's father, had somehow got to hear of Nancy's misfortunes. Instead of turning from her, they had taken her and her cause in hand, and had settled her and her three children in a general shop in Hampshire near to themselves, where she was already beginning to earn enough for a good living. The man who was the cause of all the mischief had emigrated, and meant never to return to Europe.

And Leah had taken my advice in the matter, and disclosed all to Watts. He was not in the least put out by it, as she had feared he would be; only told her she was a simpleton for not having told him before.

CHAPTER VII.
WITH MR. JONES

MY DEAR CHARLES,—I particularly wish you to come to me. I want some legal advice, and I would rather you acted for me than anyone else. Come up this morning, please.

"Your affectionate sister,

"BLANCHE."

The above note, brought from Gloucester Place on Monday morning by one of Lady Level's servants, reached me before ten o'clock. By the dashing character of the handwriting, I judged that Blanche had not been in the calmest temper when she penned it.

"Is Lord Level at home?" I inquired of the man Sanders.

"No, sir. His lordship went down to Marshdale yesterday evening. A telegram came for him, and I think it was in consequence of that he went."

I wrote a few words to Blanche, telling her I would be with her as soon as I could, and sent it by Sanders.

But a lawyer's time is not always his own. One client after another kept coming in that morning, as if on purpose; and it was half-past twelve in the day when I reached Gloucester Place.

The house in Gloucester Place was, and had been for some little time now, entirely rented by Lord Level of Major Carlen. The Major, when in London, had rooms in Seymour Street, but lived chiefly at his club.

"Her ladyship has gone out, sir," was Sanders's greeting to me, when he answered my ring at the door-bell.

"Gone out?"

"Just gone," confirmed Major Carlen, who was there, it seemed, and came forward in the wake of Sanders. "Come in, Charles."

He turned into the dining-room, and I after him. "Blanche ought to have waited in," I remarked. "I have come up at the greatest inconvenience."

"She has gone off in a tantrum," cried the Major, lowering his voice as he carefully closed the door and pushed a chair towards me, just as if the house were still in his occupancy.

"But where has she gone?" I asked, not taking the chair, but standing with my elbow on the mantelpiece.

"Who's to know? To you, in Essex Street, I shouldn't wonder. She was on the heights of impatience at your not coming."

"Not to Essex Street, I think, Major. I should have seen her."

"Nonsense! There's fifty turnings and windings between this and Essex Street, where you might miss one another; your cab taking the straight way and she the crooked," retorted the Major. "When Blanche gets her back up, you can't easily put it down."

"Something has gone contrary, I expect."

"Nothing has gone contrary but herself," replied the Major, who seemed in a cross and contrary mood on his own part. "Women are the very deuce for folly."

"Well, what is it all about, sir? I suppose you can tell me?"

The Major sat down in Lord Level's easy-chair, pushed back his cloak, and prepared to explain.

"What it's all about is just nothing, Charles; but so far as Madam Blanche's version goes, it is this," said he. "They were about to sit down, yesterday evening, to dinner—which they take on Sundays at five o'clock (good, pious souls!), and limit their fare to roast beef and a tart—when a telegram arrived from Marshdale. My lord seemed put out about it; my lady was no doubt the same. 'I must go down at once, Blanche,' said he, speaking on the spur of the moment. 'But why? Where's the need of it?' returned she. 'Surely there can be nothing at Marshdale to call you away on Sunday and in this haste?' 'Yes,' said he, 'there is; there's illness.' And then, Blanche says, he tried to cough down the words, as if he had made a slip of the tongue. 'Who is ill?' said Blanche. 'Let me see the telegram.' Level slid the telegram into his pocket, and told her it was Mr. Edwards, the old steward. Down he sat again at the table, swallowed a mouthful of beef, sent Sanders to put up a few things in his small portmanteau, and was off in a cab like the wind. Fact is," added the Major, "had he failed to catch that particular train, he would not have got down at all, being Sunday; and Sanders says that catching it must have been a near shave for his lordship."

"Is that all?"

"No. This morning there was delivered here a letter for his lordship; postmark Marshdale, handwriting a certain Italian one that Blanche has seen before. She has seen the writer, too, it seems—a fair lady called Nina. Blanche argues that as the letter came from Marshdale, the lady must be at

Marshdale, and she means to know without delay, she says, who and what this damsel is, and what the tie may be that binds her to Lord Level and gives her the right to pursue him, as she does, and the power to influence his movements, and to be at her beck and call. The probability is," added the shrewd Major, "that this person wrote to him on the Saturday, but, being a foreigner, was not aware that he would not receive her letter on Sunday morning. Finding that he did not arrive at Marshdale on the Sunday, and the day getting on, she despatched the telegram. That's how I make it out, Charles; I don't know if I am right."

"You think, then, that some Italian lady is at Marshdale?"

"Sure of it," returned the Major. "I've heard of it before to-day. Expect she lives there, making journeys to her own land between whiles, no doubt. The best and the worst of us get homesick."

"You mean that she lives there in—in—well, in a manner not quite orthodox, and that Lord Level connives at it?"

"Connives at it!" echoed the old reprobate. "Why, he is at the top and bottom of it. Level's a man of the world, always was, and does as the world does. And that little ignorant fool, Blanche, ferrets out some inkling of this, and goes and sets up a fuss! Level's as good a husband to her as can be, and yet she's not content! Commend me to foolish women! They are all alike!"

In his indignation against women in general, Major Carlen rose from his chair and began striding up and down the room. I was pondering on what he had said to me.

"What right have wives to rake up particulars of their husbands' private affairs?" he demanded fiercely. "If Level does go off to Marshdale for a few days' sojourn now and again, is it any business of Blanche's what he goes for, or what he does there, or whom he sees? Suppose he chose to maintain a whole menagerie of—of—Italian monkeys there, ought Blanche to interfere and make bones over it?"

"But——"

"He does not offend her; he does not allow her to see that anything exists to offend her: why, then, should she suspect this and suspect that, and peep and peer after Level as if she were a detective told off expressly to watch his movements?" continued the angry man. "Only an ignorant girl would dream of doing it. I am sick of her folly."

"Well now, Major Carlen, will you listen to me for a moment?" I said, speaking quietly and calmly as an antidote to his heat. "I don't believe this. I think you and Blanche are both mistaken."

He brought himself to an anchor on the hearthrug, and stared at me under his thick, grizzled eyebrows. "What is it that you don't believe, Charles?"

"This that you insinuate about Marshdale. I have faith in Lord Level; I like Lord Level; and I think you are misjudging him."

"Oh, indeed!" responded the Major. "I suppose you know what a wild blade Level always was?"

"In his early days he may have been. But you may depend upon it that when he married he left his wild ways behind him."

"All right, young Charles. And, upon my word, you are pretty near as young in the world's depths as Blanche herself is," was the Major's sarcastic remark. "Do you wish to tell me there's nothing up at Marshdale, with all these mysterious telegrams to Level, and his scampers back in answer? Come!"

"I admit that there seems to be some mystery at Marshdale. Something that we do not understand, and that Lord Level does not intend us to understand; but I must have further proof before I can believe it is of any such nature as you hint it, Major. For a long time past, Lord Level has appeared to me like a man in trouble; as if he had some anxiety on his mind."

"Well," acquiesced the Major equably, "and what can trouble a man's mind more than the exactions of these foreign syrens? Let them be Italian, or Spanish, or French—what you will—they'll worry your life out of you in the long-run. What does that Italian girl do at Marshdale?"

"I cannot say. For my own part I do not know that one is there. But if she be, if there be a whole menagerie of Italian ladies there, as you have just expressed it, Major——"

"I said a menagerie of monkeys," he growled.

"Monkeys, then. But whether they be monkeys or whether they be ladies, I feel convinced that Lord Level is acting no unworthy part—that he is loyal to his wife."

"You had better tell her so," nodded the Major; "perhaps she'll believe you. I told her the opposite. I told her that when women marry gay and attractive men, they must look out for squalls, and learn to shut their eyes a bit in going through life. I bade her bottle up her fancies, and let Marshdale and her husband alone, and not show herself a simpleton before the public."

"What did she say to that?"

"Say? It was that piece of advice which raised the storm. She burst out of the room like a maniac, declaring she wouldn't remain in it to listen to me. The next thing was, I heard the street-door bang, and saw my lady go out, putting on her gloves as she went. You came up two minutes afterwards."

I was buried in thought again. He stood staring at me, as if I had no business to have any thought.

"Look here, Major: one thing strikes me forcibly: the very fact of Lord Level allowing these telegrams to come to him openly is enough to prove that matters are not as you and Blanche suspect. If——"

"How can a telegram come secretly?" interrupted the Major.

"He would take care that they did not come at all—to his house."

"Oh, would he?" cried the old reprobate. "I should like to know how he could hinder it if any she-fiend chooses to send them."

"Rely upon it he would hinder it. Level is not one to be coerced against his will by either man or woman. Have you any idea how long Blanche will remain out?"

"Just as much as you have, Charley. She may remain away till night, for all I know."

It was of no use, then, my staying longer; and time, that day, was almost as precious to me as gold. Major Carlen threw on his cloak, and we went out together.

"I should not wonder if my young lady has gone to Seymour Street," remarked the Major. "The thought has just occurred to me."

"To your lodgings, you mean?" I asked, thinking it very unlikely.

"Yes; Mrs. Guy is there. The poor old thing arrived from Jersey on Saturday. She has come over on her usual errand—to consult the doctors; grows more ridiculously fanciful as she grows older. You might just look in upon her now, Charles; it's close by: and then you'll see whether Blanche is there or not."

I spared a few minutes for it. Poor Mrs. Guy looked very poorly indeed; but she was meek and mild as ever, and burst into tears as I greeted her. Her ailments I promised to go and hear all about another time. Yes, Blanche was there. When we went in, she was laughing at something Mrs. Guy had said, and her indignation seemed to have subsided.

I could not stay long. Blanche came out with me, thinking I should go back with her to Gloucester Place. But that was impossible; I had already wasted more time than I could well spare. Blanche was vexed.

"My dear, you should not have gone out when you were expecting me. You know how very much I am occupied."

"Papa vexed me, and drove me to it," she answered. "He said—oh, such wicked things, that I could not and would not stay to listen. And all the while I knew it was not that he believed them, but that he wanted to make excuses for Lord Level."

I did not contradict her. Let her retain, and she could, some little veneration for her step-father.

"Charles, I want to have a long conversation with you, so you must come to me as soon as you can," she said. "I mean to have a separation from my husband; perhaps a divorce, and I want you to tell me how I must proceed in it. I did think of applying to Jennings and Ward, Lord Level's solicitors, but, perhaps, you will be best."

I laughed. "You don't suppose, do you, Blanche, that Lord Level's solicitors would act for you against him."

"Now, Charles, you are speaking lightly; you are making game of me. Why do you laugh? I can tell you it is more serious than you may think for! and I am serious. I have talked of this for a long time, and now I *will* act. How shall I begin?"

"Do not begin at all, Blanche," I said, with earnestness. "*Do nothing.* Were your father living—were your mother living, they would both give you this advice—and this is not the first time I have enjoined it on you. Ah, my dear, you do not know—you little guess what misery to the wife such a climax as this which you propose would involve."

Blanche had turned to the railings round the interior of Portman Square, and halted there, apparently looking at the shrubs. Her eyes were full of tears.

"On the other hand, Charles, you do not know, you cannot guess, what I have to bear—what a misery it makes of my life."

"Are you *sure* of the facts that make the misery?"

"Why, of course I am."

"I think not, Blanche. I think you are mistaken."

She turned to me in surprise. "But I *can't* be mistaken," she said. "How can I be? If Lord Level does not go to Marshdale to—to—to see people, what does he go for?"

"He may go for something quite different. My dear, I have more confidence in your husband than you have, and I think you are wrong. I must be off; I've not another moment; but these are my last words to you, Blanche.—Take no action. Be still. *Do nothing.*"

By half-past four o'clock, the most pressing of my work was over for the day, and then I took a cab to Lincoln's Inn to see Mr. Serjeant Stillingfar. He had often said to me, good old uncle that he was: "Come to me always, Charles, when you are in any legal doubt or difficulty, or deem that my opinion may be of use to you." I was in one of those difficulties now. Some remarkably troublesome business had been laid before me by a client; I could not see my way in it at all, and was taking it to Serjeant Stillingfar.

The old chambers were just as they used to be; as they were on the day which the reader has heard of, when I saw them for the first time. Running up the stairs, there sat a clerk at the desk in the narrow room, where young Lake, full of impudence, had sat that day, Mr. Jones's empty place beside it now, as it was then.

"Is the Serjeant in?" I asked the clerk.

"No, sir; he's not out of Court yet. Mr. Jones is in."

I went on to the inner room. Old Jones, the Serjeant's own especial clerk, was writing at his little desk in the corner. Nothing was changed; not even old Jones himself. He was not, to appearance, a day older, and not an ounce bigger. Lake used to tell him he would make his fortune if he went about the country in a caravan and called himself a consumptive lamp-post.

"My uncle is not back from Court, Graham says," I observed to the clerk, after shaking hands.

"Not yet," he answered. "I don't think he'll be long. Sit down, Mr. Strange."

I took the chair I had taken that first day years ago, and waited. Mr. Jones finished the writing he was about, arranged his papers, and then came and stood with his back to the fire, having kept his quill in his hand. It must be a very hot day indeed which did not see a fire in that grate.

"If the Serjeant is not back speedily, I think I must open my business to you, and get your opinion, Mr. Jones," I said. "I dare say you could give me one as well as he."

"Some complicated case that you can't quite manage?" he rejoined.

"It's the most complicated, exasperating case I nearly ever had brought to me," I answered. "I think it is a matter more for a detective officer to deal with than a solicitor. If Serjeant Stillingfar says the same, I shall throw it up."

"Curious things, some of those detective cases," remarked Mr. Jones, gently waving his pen.

"They are. I wouldn't have to deal with them, *as* a detective, for the world. Shall I relate this case to you?"

He took out his watch and looked at it. "Better wait a bit longer, Mr. Charles. I expect the Serjeant every minute now."

"Don't you wonder that my uncle continues to work?" I cried presently. "He is old now. *I* should retire."

"He is sixty-five. If you were not young yourself, you would not call that old."

"Old enough, I should say, for work to be a labour to him."

"A labour that he loves, and that he is as capable of performing as he was twenty years ago," returned old Jones. "No, Mr. Charles, I do not wonder that he should continue to work."

"Did you know that he had been offered a judgeship?"

Old Jones laughed a little. I thought it was as much as to say there was little which concerned the Serjeant that he did not know.

"He has been offered a judgeship more than once—had it pressed upon him, Mr. Charles. The last time was when Mr. Baron Charlton died."

"Why! that is only a month or two ago!"

"Just about nine weeks, I fancy."

"And he declined it?"

"He declines them all."

"But what can be his motive? It would give him more rest than he enjoys now——"

"I don't altogether know that," interrupted the clerk. "The judges are very much over-worked now. It would increase his responsibility; and he is one to feel that, perhaps painfully."

"You mean when he had to pass the dread sentence of death. A new judge must always feel that at the beginning."

"I heard one of our present judges say—it was in this room, too, Mr. Charles—that the first time he put on the black cap he never closed his eyes the whole night after it. All the Bench are not so sensitive as that, you know."

A thought suddenly struck me. "Surely," I cried, "you do not mean that *that* is the reason for my uncle's refusing a seat on the Bench!"

"Not at all. He'd get over that in time, as others do. Oh no! that has nothing to do with it."

"Then I really cannot see what can have to do with it. It would give him a degree of rest; yes, it would; and it would give him rank and position."

"But it would take from him half his income. Yes, just about half, I reckon," repeated Mr. Jones, attentively regarding the feather of the pen.

"What of that? He must be putting by heaps and heaps of money—and he has neither wife nor child to put by for."

"Ah!" said the clerk, "that is just how we all are apt to judge of a neighbour's business. Would it surprise you very much, sir, if I told you that the Serjeant is *not* putting by?"

"But he must be putting by. Or what becomes of his money?"

"He spends it, Mr. Charles."

"*Spends it!* Upon what?"

"Upon other people."

Mr. Jones looked at me from across the hearthrug, and I looked at him. The assertion puzzled me.

"It's true," he said with a nod. "You have not forgotten that great calamity which happened some ten or twelve years ago, Mr. Charles? That bank which went to pieces, and broke up homes and hearts? *Your* money went in it."

As if I could forget that!

"The Serjeant's money, all he had then saved, went in it," continued the clerk. "Mortifying enough, of course, but he was in the full swing of his prosperity, and could soon have replaced it. What he could not so easily replace, Mr. Charles, was the money he had been the means of placing in the bank belonging to other people, and which was lost. He had done it for the best. He held the bank to be thoroughly sound and prosperous; he could not have had more confidence in his own integrity than he had in that bank; and he had counselled friends and others whom he knew, who were not as well off as he was, to invest all they could spare in it, believing he was doing them a kindness. Instead of that, it ruined them."

I thought I saw what the clerk was coming to. After a pause, he went on:

"It is these people that he has been working for, Mr. Charles. Some of them he has entirely repaid—the money, you know, which he caused them to lose. He considered it his duty to recompense them, so far as he could; and to keep them, where they needed to be kept, until he had effected that. For those who were better off and did not need present help, he put money by as he could spare it, investing it in the funds in their name: I dare say your name is amongst them. That's what Mr. Serjeant Stillingfar does with his income, and that's why he keeps on working."

I had never suspected this.

"I believe it is almost accomplished now," said the clerk. "So nearly that I thought he might, perhaps, have taken the judgeship on this last occasion. But he did not. 'Just a few months longer in harness, Jones,' he said to me, 'and then——?' So I reckon that we shall yet see him on the Bench, Mr. Charles."

"He must be very good."

"Good!" echoed old Jones, with emotion; "he is made of goodness. There are few people like him. He would help the whole world if he could. I don't believe there's any man who has ever done a single service for him of the most trifling nature but he would wish to place beyond the reach of poverty. 'I've put a trifle by for you, Jones,' he said to me the other day, 'in case you might be at a loss for another such place as this when my time's over.' And when I tried to thank him——"

Mr. Jones broke down. Bringing the quill pen under his eyes, as if he suddenly caught sight of a flaw thereon, I saw a drop of water fall on to it.

"Yes, Mr. Charles, he said that to me. It has taken a load from my mind. When a man is on the downhill of life and is not sure of his future, he can't help being anxious. The Serjeant has paid me a liberal salary, as you may well guess, but he knows that it has not been in my power to put by a fraction of it. 'You are too generous with your money, Serjeant,' I said to him one day, a good while ago. 'Ah no, Jones, not at all,' he answered. 'God has prospered me so marvellously in these later years, what can I do but strive to prosper others?' Those were his very words."

And with these last words of Jones's our conference came to an end. The door was abruptly thrown open by Graham to admit the Serjeant. Mr.

Jones helped him off with his wig and gown, and handed him the little flaxen top that he wore when not on duty. Then Jones, leaving the room for a few moments, came back with a glass of milk, which he handed to his master.

"Would not a glass of wine do you more good, uncle?" I asked.

"No, lad; not so much. A glass of milk after a hard day's work in Court refreshes me. I never touch wine except at a dinner. I take a little then; not much."

Sitting down together when Mr. Jones had again left us, I opened my business to the Serjeant as concisely as possible. He listened attentively, but made no remark until the end.

"Now go over it all again, Charles." I did so: and this second time I was repeatedly interrupted by remarks or questions. After that we discussed the case.

"I cannot see any reason why you should not take up the matter," he said, when he had given it a little silent consideration. "I do not look upon it quite as you do; I think you have formed a wrong judgment. It is intricate at present; I grant you that; but if you proceed in the manner I have suggested, you will unravel it."

"Thank you, Uncle Stillingfar. I can never thank you enough for all your kindness to me."

"Were you so full of anxiety over this case?" he asked, as we were shaking hands, and I was about to leave. "You look as though you had a weight of it on your brow."

"And so I have, uncle; but not about this case. Something nearer home."

"What *is* it?" he returned, looking at me.

"It is—— Perhaps I had better not tell it you."

"I understand," he slowly said. "Tom Heriot, I suppose. Why does he not get away?"

"He is too ill for that at present: confined to his room and his bed. Of course, he does not run quite so great a risk as he did when he persisted in parading the streets, but danger is always imminent."

"He ought to end the danger by getting away. Very ill, is he?"

"So ill that I think danger will soon be all at an end in another way; it certainly will be unless he rallies."

"What is the matter with him?"

"I cannot help fearing that consumption has set in."

"Poor fellow! Oh, Charles, how that fine young man has spoilt his life! Consumption?—Wait a bit—let me think," broke off the Serjeant. "Why, yes, I remember now; it was consumption that Colonel Heriot's first wife died of—Tom's mother."

"Tom said so the last time I saw him."

"Ah. He knows it, then. Better not see him too often, Charles. You are running a risk yourself, as you must be aware."

"Yes; I know I am. It is altogether a trial. Good-day, uncle."

I shook hands with Jones as I passed through his room, and ran down the stairs, feeling all the better for my interview with him and with his patron, Mr. Serjeant Stillingfar.

CHAPTER VIII.
AN ACCIDENT.

THE drawing-room floor at Lennard's made very comfortable quarters for Tom Heriot, and his removal from the room in Southwark had been accomplished without difficulty. Mrs. Lennard, a patient, mild, weak woman, who could never have been strong-minded, made him an excellent nurse, her more practical and very capable daughter, Charlotte, aiding her when necessary.

A safer refuge could not have been found in London. The Lennards were so often under a cloud themselves as regarded pecuniary matters, so beset at times by their unwelcome creditors—the butcher, baker and grocer—that the chain of their front door was kept habitually fastened, and no one was admitted within its portals without being first of all subjected to a comprehensive survey. Had some kind friend made a rush to the perambulating policeman of the district, to inform him that the domicile of those Lennards was again in a state of siege, he would simply have speculated upon whether the enemy was this time the landlord or the Queen's taxes. It chanced to be neither; but it was well for the besieged to favour the impression that it was one or the other, or both. Policemen do not wage war with unfortunate debtors, and Mr. Lennard's house was as safe as a remote castle.

"Mr. Brown" Tom was called there; none of the household, with the exception of its master, having any idea that it was not his true name. "One of the gentlemen clerks in Essex Street, who has no home in London; I have undertaken to receive him while he is ill," Mr. Lennard had carelessly remarked to his wife and daughters before introducing Tom. They had unsuspecting minds, except as regarded their own creditors, those ladies—ladies always, though fallen from their former state—and never thought to question the statement, or to be at all surprised that Mr. Strange himself took an interest in his clerk's illness, and paid an evening visit to him now and then. The doctor who was called in, a hard-worked practitioner named Purfleet, did his best for "Mr. Brown," but had no time to spare for curiosity about him in any other way, or to give so much as a thought to his antecedents.

And just at first, after being settled at Lennard's, Tom Heriot seemed to be taking a turn for the better. The warmth of the comfortable rooms, the care given to him, the strengthening diet, and perhaps a feeling that he was in a safer asylum than he had yet found, all had their effect upon him for good.

"Hatch!" called out Mrs. Brightman.

Hatch ran in from the next room. "Yes, ma'am."

"Let Perry go and tell the gardener to cut some of his best grapes, white and purple, and do you arrange them in a basket. I shall go up to Essex Street and see my daughter this afternoon, and will take them to her. Order the carriage for half-past two o'clock."

"Miss Annabel will be finely pleased to see you, ma'am!" remarked Hatch.

"Possibly so. But she is no longer Miss Annabel. Go and see about the grapes."

When Mrs. Brightman's tones were cold and haughty, and they sounded especially so just now, she brooked no dilatoriness in those who had to obey her behests. Hatch turned away immediately, and went along talking to herself.

"She's getting cross and restless again. I'm certain of it. In a week's time from this we shall have her as bad as before. And for ever so many weeks now she has been as cautious and sober as a judge! Hang the drink, then! Doctors may well call it a disease when it comes to this stage with people. Here—I say, Perry!"

The butler, passing along the hall, heard Hatch's call, and stopped. She gave her cap-strings a fling backwards as she advanced to him.

"You are to go and tell Church to cut a basket of grapes, and to mix 'em, white and black. The very best and ripest that is in the greenhouse; they be for Miss Annabel."

"All right, I'll go at once," answered Perry. "But you need not snap a man's nose off, Hatch, or look as if you were going to eat him. What has put you out?"

"Enough has put me out; and you might know that, old Perry, if you had any sense," retorted Hatch. "When do I snap people's noses off—which it's my tone, I take it, that you mean—except I'm that bothered and worried I can't speak sweet?"

"Well, what's amiss?" asked Perry.

They were standing close together, and Hatch lowered her voice to a whisper. "The missis is going off again; I be certain sure on't."

"*No!*" cried Perry, full of dismay. "But, look here, Hatch"—suddenly diving into one of his jackets—"she can't have done it; here's the cellar-key. I can be upon my word that there's not a drain of anything out."

"You always did have the brains of a turkey, you know, Perry," was Hatch's gracious rejoinder; "and I'm tired of reminding you of it. Who said missis had took anything? Not me. She haven't—yet. As you observe, there's nothing up for her to take. But she'll be ordering you to bring something up before to-morrow's over; perhaps before to-day is."

"Dear, dear!" lamented the faithful servant. "Don't you think you may be mistaken, Hatch? What do you judge by?"

"I judge by herself. I've not lived with my missis all these years without learning to notice signs and tokens. Her manner to-day and her restlessness is just as plain as the sun in the sky. I know what it means, and you'll know it too, as soon as she gives you her orders to unlock the cellar."

"Can nothing be done?" cried the unhappy Perry. "Could I *lose* the key of the cellar, do you think, Hatch? Would that be of any good?"

"It would hold good just as long as you'd be in getting a hammer and poker to break it open with; you've not got to deal with a pack of schoolboys that's under control," was Hatch's sarcastic reproof. "But I think there's one thing we might try, Perry, and that is, run round to Mr. Close and tell him about it. Perhaps he could give her something to stop the craving."

"I'll go," said Perry. "I'll slip round when I've told Church about the grapes."

"And the carriage is ordered early—half-past two; so mind you are in readiness," concluded Hatch.

Perry went to the surgeon's, after delivering his orders to the gardener. But Mr. Close was not at home, and the man came away again without leaving any message; he did not choose to enter upon the subject with Mr. Dunn, the assistant. The latter inquired who was ill, and Perry replied that nobody was; he had only come to speak a private word to Mr. Close, which could wait. In point of fact, he meant to call later.

But the curiosity of Mr. Dunn, who was a very inquisitive young man, fonder of attending to other people's business than of doing his own, had been aroused by this. He considered Perry's manner rather mysterious, as well as the suppression of the message, and he enlarged upon the account to Mr. Close when he came in. Mr. Close made no particular rejoinder; but in his own mind he felt little doubt that Mrs. Brightman was breaking out again, and determined to go and see her when he had had his dinner.

Perry returned home, and waited on his mistress at luncheon, quaking inwardly all the time, as he subsequently confessed to Hatch, lest she should ask him for something that was not upon the table. However, she did not do so; but she was very restless, as Perry observed; ate little, drank no water, and told Perry to bring her a cup of coffee.

At half-past two the carriage stood at the gate, the silver on the horses' harness glittering in the sun. Quickly enough appeared the procession from the house. Mrs. Brightman, upright and impassive, walking with stately step; Hatch, a shawl or two upon her arm, holding an umbrella over her mistress to shade her from the sun; Perry in the background, carrying the basket of grapes. Perry would attend his mistress in her drive, as usual, but not Hatch.

The servants were placing the shawls and the grapes in the carriage, and Mrs. Brightman, who hated anything to be done after she had taken her seat, was waiting to enter it, when Mr. Close, the surgeon, came bustling up.

"Going for a drive this fine day!" he exclaimed, as he shook hands with Mrs. Brightman. "I'm glad of that. I had been thinking that perhaps you were not well."

"Why should you think so?" asked she.

"Well, Perry was round at my place this morning, and left a message that he wanted to see me. I——"

Mr. Close suppressed the remainder of his speech as his gaze suddenly fell on Perry's startled face. The man had turned from the carriage, and was looking at him in helpless, beseeching terror. A faithful retainer was Perry, an honest butler; but at a pinch his brains were no better than what Hatch had compared them with—those of a turkey.

Mrs. Brightman, her countenance taking its very haughtiest expression, gazed first at the doctor, then at Perry, as if demanding what this might mean; possibly, poor lady, she had a suspicion of it. But Hatch, ready Hatch, was equal to the occasion: *she* never lost her presence of mind.

"I told Perry he might just as well have asked young Mr. Dunn for 'em, when he came back without the drops," said she, facing the surgeon and speaking carelessly. "Your not being in didn't matter. It was some cough-drops I sent him for; the same as those you've let us have before, Mr. Close. Our cook's cough is that bad, she can't sleep at night, nor let anybody else sleep that's within earshot of her room."

"Well, I came round in a hurry, thinking some of you might be suffering from this complaint that's going about," said Mr. Close, taking up the clue in an easy manner.

"That there spasadic cholera," assented Hatch.

"Cholera! It's not cholera. There's nothing of that sort about," said the surgeon. "But there's a good bit of influenza; I have half a dozen patients suffering from it. A spell of bright weather such as this, though, will soon drive it away. And I'll send you some of the drops when I get back, Hatch."

Mrs. Brightman advanced to the carriage; the surgeon was at hand to assist her in. Perry stood on the other side his mistress. Hatch had retreated to the gate and was looking on.

Suddenly a yell, as of something unearthly, startled their ears. A fierce-looking bull, frightened probably by the passers-by on the road, and the prods given to it by the formidable stick of its driver, had dashed behind the carriage on to the foot-path, and set up that terrible roar. Mr. Close looked round, Perry did the same; whilst Mrs. Brightman, who was in the very act of getting into her carriage, and whose nerves were more sensitive than theirs, turned sharply round also and screamed.

Again Hatch came to the rescue. She had closed the umbrella and lodged it against the pillar of the gate, for here they were under the shade of trees. Seizing the umbrella now, she opened it with a great dash and noise, and rushed towards the bull, pointing it menacingly. The animal, no doubt more startled than they were, tore away and gained the highroad again. Then everyone had leisure to see that Mrs. Brightman was lying on the ground partly under the carriage.

She must have fallen in turning round, partly from fright, partly from the moving of the carriage. The horses had also been somewhat startled by the bull's noise, and one of them began to prance. The coachman had his horses well in hand, and soon quieted them; but he had not been able to prevent the movement, which had no doubt chiefly caused his mistress to fall.

They quickly drew her from under the carriage and attempted to raise her; but she cried out with such tones of agony that the surgeon feared she was seriously injured. As soon as possible she was conveyed indoors on a mattress. Another surgeon joined Mr. Close, and it was found that her leg was broken near the ankle.

When it had been set and the commotion was subsiding, Perry was despatched to Essex Street with the carriage and the bad news—the carriage to bring back Annabel.

"What was it you really came to my surgery for, Perry?" Mr. Close took an opportunity of asking him before he started.

"It was about my mistress, sir," answered the man. "Hatch felt quite sure, by signs and tokens, that Mrs. Brightman was going to—to—be ill again. She sent me to tell you, sir, and to ask if you couldn't give her something to stop it."

"Ah, I thought as much. But when I saw you all out there, your mistress looking well and about to take a drive, I concluded I had been mistaken," said the surgeon.

I had run upstairs during the afternoon to ask a question of Annabel, and was standing beside her at the drawing-room window, where she sat at work, when a carriage came swiftly down the street, and stopped at the door.

"Why, it is mamma's!" exclaimed Annabel, looking out.

"But I don't see her in it," I rejoined.

"Oh, she must be in it, Charles. Perry is on the box."

Perry was getting down, but was not quite so quick in his movements as a slim young footman would be. He rang the door-bell, and I was fetched down to him. In two minutes afterwards I had disclosed the news to my wife, and brought Perry upstairs that she might herself question him. The tears were coursing down her cheeks.

"Don't take on, Miss Annabel," said the man, feeling quite too much lost in the bad tidings to remember Annabel's new title. "There's not the least bit of danger, ma'am; Mr. Close bade me say it; all is sure to go on well."

"Did you bring the carriage for me, Perry?"

"Yes, ma'am, I did. And it was my mistress herself thought of it. When Mr. Close, or Hatch—one of 'em it was, I don't know which—told her they were going to send me for you, she said, 'Let Perry take the carriage.' Oh, ma'am, indeed she is fully as well as she could be: it was only at first that she seemed faintish like."

Annabel went back in the carriage at once. I promised to follow her as early in the evening as I could get away. Relying upon the butler's assurance that Mrs. Brightman was not in the slightest danger; that, on the contrary, it would be an illness of weeks, if not of months, there was no necessity for accompanying Annabel at an inconvenient moment.

"It is, in one sense, the luckiest thing that could have happened to her," Mr. Close remarked to me that evening when we were conversing together.

"Lucky! How do you mean?"

"Well, she *must* be under our control now," he answered in significant tones, "and we were fearing, only to-day, that she was on the point of breaking out again. A long spell of enforced abstinence, such as this, may effect wonders."

Of course, looking at it in that light, the accident might be called fortunate. "There's a silver lining to every cloud."

Annabel took up her abode temporarily at her mother's: Mrs. Brightman requested it. I went down there of an evening—though not every evening—returning to Essex Street in the morning. Tom's increasing illness kept me in town occasionally, for I could not help going to see him, and he was growing weaker day by day. The closing features of consumption were gaining upon him rapidly. To add to our difficulties, Mr. Policeman Wren, who seemed to follow Tom's changes of domicile in a very ominous and remarkable manner, had now transferred his beat from Southwark, and might be seen pacing before Lennard's door ten times a day.

One morning when I had come up from Clapham and was seated in my own room opening letters, Lennard entered. He closed the door with a quiet, cautious movement, and waited, without speaking.

"Anything particular, Lennard?"

"Yes, sir; I've brought rather bad news," he said. "Captain Heriot is worse."

"Worse? In what way? But he is not Captain Heriot, Lennard; he is Mr. Brown. Be careful."

"We cannot be overheard," he answered, glancing at the closed door. "He appeared so exceedingly weak last night that I thought I would sit up with him for an hour or two, and then lie down on his sofa for the rest of the night. About five o'clock this morning he had a violent fit of coughing and broke a blood-vessel."

"What did you do?"

"I know a little of the treatment necessary in such cases, and we got the doctor to him as soon as possible. Mr. Purfleet does not give the slightest hope now. In fact, he thinks that a very few days more will bring the ending."

I sat back in my chair. Poor Tom! Poor Tom!

"It is the best for him, Mr. Charles," spoke Lennard, with some emotion. "Better, infinitely, than that of which he has been running the risk. When a man's life is marred as he has marred his, heaven must seem like a haven of refuge to him."

"Has he any idea of his critical state?"

"Yes; and, I feel sure, is quite reconciled to it. He remarked this morning how much he should like to see Blanche: meaning, I presume, Lady Level."

"Ah, but there are difficulties in the way, Lennard. I will come to him myself, but not until evening. There's no immediate danger, you tell me, and I do not care to be seen entering your house during the day while he is in it. The big policeman might be on the watch, and ask me what I wanted there."

Lennard left the room and I returned to my letters. The next I took up was a note from Blanche. Lord Level was not *yet* back from Marshdale, she told me in it; he kept writing miserable scraps of notes in which he put her off with excuses from day to day, always assuring her he hoped to be up on the morrow. But she could see she was being played with; and the patience which, in obedience to me and Major Carlen, she had been exercising, was very nearly exhausted. She wrote this, she concluded by saying, to warn me that it was so.

Truth to say, I did wonder what was keeping Level at Marshdale. He had been there more than a week now.

CHAPTER IX.
LAST DAYS.

TOM HERIOT lay on his sofa in his bedroom, the firelight flickering on his faded face. This was Monday, the third day since the attack spoken of by Lennard, and there had not been any return of it. His voice was stronger this evening; he seemed better altogether, and was jesting, as he loved to do. Leah had been to see him during the day, and he was recounting one or two of their passages-at-arms, with much glee.

"Charley, old fellow, you look as solemn as a judge."

Most likely I did. I sat on the other side the hearthrug, gazing as I listened to him; and I thought I saw in his face the grayness that frequently precedes death.

"Did you know that that giant of the force, Wren, had his eye upon me, Charley?"

"No! Why do you say so?"

"Well, I think he has—some suspicion, at any rate. He parades before the house like a walking apparition. I look at him from behind the curtains in the other room. He paraded in like manner, you know, before that house in Southwark and the other one in Lambeth."

"It may be only a coincidence, Tom. The police are moved about a good deal from beat to beat, I fancy."

"Perhaps so," assented Tom carelessly. "If he came in and took me, I don't think he could do much with me now. He accosted Purfleet to-day."

"Accosted Purfleet!"

Tom nodded. "After his morning visit to me, he went dashing out of the street-door in his usual quick way, and dashed against Wren. One might think a regiment of soldiers were always waiting to have their legs and arms cut off, and that Purfleet had to do it, by the way he rushes about," concluded Tom.

"Well?"

"'In a hurry this morning, doctor,' says old Wren, who is uncommonly fond of hearing himself talk. 'And who is it that's ill at Mr. Lennard's?' 'I generally am in a hurry,' says Purfleet, 'and so would you be if you had as many sick people on your hands. At Lennard's? Why, that poor suffering daughter of his has had another attack, and I don't know whether I shall save her.' And, with that, Purfleet got away. He related this to me when he came in at tea-time."

A thought struck me. "But, Tom, does Purfleet know that you are in concealment here? Or why should he have put his visits to you upon Maria Lennard?"

"Why, how could he be off knowing it? Lennard asked him at first, as a matter of precaution, not to speak of me in the neighbourhood. Mr. Brown was rather under a cloud just now, he said. I wouldn't mind betting a silver sixpence, Charley, that he knows I am Tom Heriot."

I wondered whether Tom was joking.

"Likely enough," went on Tom. "He knows that you come to see me, and that you are Mr. Strange, of Essex Street. And he has heard, I'll lay, that Mr. Strange had a wicked sort of half-brother, one Captain Heriot, who fell into the fetters of the law and escaped them, and—and may be the very Mr. Brown who's lying ill here. Purfleet can put two and two together as cleverly as other people, Charles."

"If so, it is frightfully hazardous——"

"Not at all," interrupted Tom with equanimity. "He'd no more betray me, Charley, than he'd betray himself. Doctors don't divulge the secrets of their patients; they keep them. It is a point of honour in the medical code: as well as of self-interest. What family would call in a man who was known to run about saying the Smiths next door had veal for dinner to-day, and they ought to have had mutton? If no more harm reaches me than any brought about by Purfleet, I am safe enough."

It might be as he said. And I saw that he would be incautious to the end.

At that moment Mrs. Lennard came in with something in a breakfast-cup. "You are a good lady," said Tom gratefully. "See how they feed me up, Charley!"

But for the hollow tones, the hectic flush and the brilliant eyes, it might almost have been thought he was getting better. The cough had nearly left him, and the weakness was not more apparent than it had been for a week past. But that faint, deep, *far-away* sounding voice, which had now come on, told the truth. The close was near at hand.

After Mrs. Lennard had left the room with the empty cup, Tom lay back on the sofa, put his head on the pillow, and in a minute or two seemed to be asleep. Presently I moved gently across the hearthrug to fold the warm, light quilt upon his knees. He opened his eyes.

"You need not creep, Charley. I am not asleep. I had a regular good sleep in the afternoon, and don't feel inclined for it now. I was thinking about the funeral."

"The funeral!" I echoed, taken back. "Whose funeral?"

"Mine. They won't care to lay me by my mother, will they?—I mean my own mother. The world might put its inquisitive word in, and say that must be Tom Heriot, the felon. Neither you nor Level would like that, nor old Carlen either."

I made no answer, uncertain what to say.

"Yet I should like to lie by her," he went on. "There was a large vault made, when she died, to hold the three of us—herself, my father and me. *They* are in it; I should like to be placed with them."

"Time enough to think of that, Tom, when—when—the time comes," I stammered.

"The time's not far off now, Charley."

"Two nights ago, when I was here, you assured me you were getting better."

"Well, I thought I might be; there are such ups and downs in a man's state. He will appear sick unto death to-day, and tomorrow be driving down to a whitebait dinner at Greenwich. I've changed my opinion, Charley; I've had my warning."

"Had your warning! What does that mean?"

"I should like to see Blanche," he whispered. "Dear little Blanche! How I used to tease her in our young days, and Leah would box my ears for it; and I teased you also, Charley. Could you not bring her here, if Level would let her come?"

"Tom, I hardly know. For one thing, she has not heard anything of the past trouble, as you are aware. She thinks you are in India with the regiment, and calls you a very undutiful brother for not writing to her. I suppose it might be managed."

"Dear little Blanche!" he repeated. "Yes, I teased her—and loved her all the time. Just one visit, Charley. It will be the last until we meet upon the eternal shores. Try and contrive it."

I sat thinking how it might be done—the revelation to Blanche, bringing her to the house, and obtaining the consent of Lord Level; for I should not care to stir in it without his consent. Tom appeared to be thinking also, and a silence ensued. It was he who broke it.

"Charles!"

"Yes?"

"Do you ever recall events that passed in our old life at White Littleham Rectory? do any of them lie in your memory?"

"I think all of them lie in it," I answered. "My memory is, you know, a remarkably good one."

"Ay," said Tom. And then he paused again. "Do you recollect that especial incident when your father told us of his dream?" he continued presently. "I picture the scene now; it has been present to my mind all day. A frosty winter morning, icicles on the trees and frosty devices on the window-panes. You and I and your father seated round the breakfast-table; Leah pouring out the coffee and cutting bread and butter for us. He appeared to be in deep thought, and when I remarked upon it, and you asked him what he was thinking of, he said his dream. D'you mind it, lad?"

"I do. The thing made an impression on me. The scene and what passed at it are as plain to me now as though it had happened yesterday. After saying he was thinking of his dream, he added, in a dubious tone, 'If it *was* a dream.' Mr. Penthorn came in whilst he was telling it.

"He was fast asleep; had gone to bed in the best of health, probably concocting matter for next Sunday's sermon," resumed Tom, recalling the facts. "Suddenly, he awoke at the sound of a voice. It was his late wife's voice; your mother, Charley. He was wide awake on the instant, and knew the voice for hers; she appeared to be standing at the bedside."

"But he did not see her," I put in.

"No; he never said he saw her," replied Tom Heriot. "But the impression was upon him that a figure stood there, and that after speaking it retreated towards the window. He got up and struck a light and found the room empty, no trace of anyone's having been in it. Nevertheless he could not get rid of the belief, though not a superstitious man, that it was his wife who came to him."

"In the spirit."

"In the spirit, of course. He knew her voice perfectly, he said. Mr. Penthorn rather ridiculed the matter; saying it was nothing but a vivid dream. I don't think it made much impression upon your father, except that it puzzled him."

"I don't think it did," I assented, my thoughts all in the past. "As you observe, Tom, he was not superstitious; he had no particular belief in the supernatural."

"No; it faded from all our minds with the day—Leah's perhaps excepted. But what was the result? On the fourth night afterwards he died. The dream occurred on the Friday morning a little before three o'clock; your father looked at his watch when he got out of bed and saw that it wanted a quarter to three. On Tuesday morning at a quarter to three he died in his study, into which he had been carried after his accident."

All true. The circumstances, to me, were painful even now.

"Well, what do you make of it, Charles?"

"Nothing. But I don't quite understand your question."

"Do you think his wife really came to him?—That she was permitted to come back to earth to warn him of his approaching death?"

"I have always believed that. I can hardly see how anyone could doubt it."

"Well, Charley, I did. I was a graceless, light-headed young wight, you know, and serious things made no impression on me. If I thought about it at all, it was to put it down to fancy; or a dream, as Mr. Penthorn said; and I don't believe I've ever had the thing in my mind from that time to this."

"And why should it come back to you now?" I asked.

"Because," answered Tom, "I think I have had a similar warning."

He spoke very calmly. I looked at him. He was sitting upright on the sofa now, his feet stretched out on a warm wool footstool, the quilt lying across his knees, and his hands resting upon it.

"What can you mean, Tom?"

"It was last night," he answered; "or, rather, this morning. I was in bed, and pretty soundly asleep, for me, and I began to dream. I thought I saw my father come in through the door, that one opening to the passage, cross the room and sit down by the bedside with his face turned to me. I mean my own father, Colonel Heriot. He looked just as he used to look; not a day older; his fine figure erect, his bright, wavy hair brushed off his brow as he always wore it, his blue eyes smiling and kindly. I was not in the least surprised to see him; his coming in seemed to be quite a matter of course. 'Well, Thomas,' he began, looking at me after he had sat down; 'we have been parted for some time, and I have much to say to you.' 'Say it now, papa,' I answered, going back in my dream to the language of childhood's days. 'There's not time now,' he replied; 'we must wait a little yet; it won't be long, Thomas.' Then I saw him rise from the chair, re-cross the room to the door, turn to look at me with a smile, and go out, leaving the door open. I awoke in a moment; at the very moment, I am certain; and for some little time I could not persuade myself that what had passed was not reality. The chair in which he had sat stood at the bedside, and the door was wide open."

"But I suppose the chair had been there all night, and that someone was sitting up with you? Whoever it was must have opened the door."

"The chair had been there all night," assented Tom. "But the door had *not* been opened by human hands, so far as I can learn. It was old Faith's turn to sit up last night—that worthy old soul of a servant who has clung to the Lennards through all their misfortunes. Finding that I slept comfortably, Faith had fallen asleep too in the big chair in that corner behind you. She declared that the door had been firmly shut—and I believe she thought it was I who had got up and opened it."

"It was a dream, Tom."

"Granted. But it was a warning. It came—nay, who can say it was not *he* who came?—to show me that I shall soon be with him. We shall have time, and to spare, to talk then. I have never had so vivid a dream in my life; or one that so left behind it the impression that it had been reality."

"Well——"

"Look here," he interrupted. "Your father said, if you remember, that the visit paid to him, whether real or imaginary, by his wife, and the words she spoke, had revived within him his recollections of her voice, which had in a slight degree begun to fade. Well, Charles, I give you my word that I had partly forgotten my father's appearance; I was only a little fellow when he died; but his visit to me in my dream last night has brought it back most vividly. Come, you wise old lawyer, what do you say to that?"

"I don't know, Tom. Such things *are*, I suppose."

"If I got well and lived to be a hundred years old, I should never laugh at them again."

"Did you tell Leah this when she was here to-day?"

"Ay; and of course she burst out crying. 'Take it as it's meant, Master Tom,' said she, 'and prepare yourself. It is your warning.' Just as she had told your father, Charles, that that other was *his* warning. She was right then; she is right now."

"You cannot know it. And you must not let this trouble you."

"It does not trouble me," he answered quickly. "Rather the contrary, for it sets my mind at rest. I have had little hope of myself for some time past; I have had none, so to say, since that sudden attack a few nights ago; nevertheless, I won't say but a grain of it may have still deluded me now and again. Hope is the last thing we part with in this world, you know, lad. But this dream-visit of my father has shown me the truth beyond all doubt; and now I have only to make my packet, as the French say, and wait for the signal to start."

We talked together a little longer, but my time was up. I left him for the night and apparently in the best of spirits.

Lennard was alone in his parlour when I got downstairs. I asked him whether he had heard of this fancy of Tom's about the dream.

"Yes," he answered. "He told me about it this evening, when I was sitting with him after tea; but he did not seem at all depressed by it. I don't think it matters much either way," added Lennard thoughtfully, "for the end cannot be far off now."

"He has an idea that Purfleet guesses who he really is."

"But he has no grounds for saying it," returned Lennard. "Purfleet heard when he was first called in that 'Mr. Brown' wished to be kept *en cachette*, if I may so put it; but that he should guess him to be Captain Heriot is quite improbable. Because Captain Heriot is aware of his own identity, he assumes that other people must needs be aware of it."

"One might trust Purfleet not to betray him, I fancy, if he does guess it?"

"That I am sure of," said Lennard warmly. "He is kind and benevolent. Most medical men are so from their frequent contact with the dark shades of life, whether of sickness or of sorrow. As to Purfleet, he is too hard-worked, poor man, to have much leisure for speculating upon the affairs of other people."

"Wren is still walking about here."

"Yes; but I think he has been put upon this beat in the ordinary way of things, not that he is looking after anyone in particular. Mr. Strange, if he had any suspicion of Captain Heriot in Lambeth, he would have taken him; he would have taken him again when in Southwark; and he would, ere this, have taken him here. Wren appears to be one of those gossiping men who must talk to everybody; and I believe that is all the mystery."

Wishing Lennard good-night, I went home to Essex Street, and sat down to write to Lord Level. He would not receive the letter at Marshdale until the following afternoon, but it would be in time for him to answer me by the evening post.

CHAPTER X.
LAST WORDS.

THE next day, Tuesday, I was very busy, hurrying forward to get down to Clapham in time for dinner in the evening. Lennard's report in the morning had been that Captain Heriot was no worse, and that Mr. Purfleet, who had paid him an early visit, said there might be no change for a week or more.

In the afternoon I received a brief note from Mr. Serjeant Stillingfar, asking me to be in Russell Square the following morning by eight o'clock: he wished to see me very particularly.

Knowing that when he named any special hour he meant it, and that he expected everyone who had dealings with him to be as punctual as himself, I came up to town on the Wednesday morning, and was at his house a few minutes before eight o'clock. The Serjeant was just sitting down to breakfast.

"Will you take some, Charles?" he asked.

"No, thank you, uncle. I have just come up from Clapham, and breakfasted before starting."

"How is Mrs. Brightman going on?"

"Quite well. It will be a long job, the doctors say, from something unusual connected with the fracture, but nothing dangerous."

"Sit down, Charles," he said. "And tell me at once. Is Captain Heriot," lowering his voice, "in a state to be got away?"

The words did not surprise me. The whole night it had been in my mind that the Serjeant's mandate concerned Tom Heriot.

"No; it would be impossible," I answered. "He has to be moved gently, from bed to sofa, and can only walk, if he attempts it at all, by being helped on both sides. Three or four days ago, a vessel on the lungs broke; any undue exertion would at once be fatal."

"Then, do I understand you that he is actually dying?"

"Undoubtedly he is, sir. I was with him on Monday night, and saw in his face the gray hue which is the precursor of death. I am sure I was not mistaken——"

"That peculiar hue can never be mistaken by those who have learnt from sad experience," he interrupted dreamily.

"He may linger on a few days, even a week or so, I believe the doctor thinks, but death is certainly on its road; and he must die where he is, Uncle Stillingfar. He cannot be again moved."

The Serjeant sat silent for a few moments. "It is very unfortunate, Charles," he resumed. "Could he have been got away it would be better for him, better for you all. Though, in truth, it is not I who ought to suggest it, as you well know; but sometimes one's private and public duties oppose each other."

"Have you heard anything, uncle?"

"I have heard from a sure source that the authorities know that Captain Heriot is in London. They know it positively: but not, I think, where he is concealed. The search for him will now commence in earnest."

"It is, indeed, unfortunate. I have been hoping he would be left to die in peace. One thing is certain: if the police find him they can only let him remain where he is. They cannot remove him."

"Then nothing can be done: things must take their course," sighed the Serjeant. "You must take precautions yourself, Charles. Most probably the movements of those connected with him will now be watched, in the hope that they may afford a clue to his hiding-place."

"I cannot abandon him, Uncle Stillingfar. I must see him to the end. We have been as brothers, you know. He wants to see Blanche, and I have written about it to Lord Level."

"Well, well, I cannot advise; I wish I could," he replied. "But I thought it my duty to let you know this."

"A few days will, in any case, see the ending," I whispered as I bade him goodbye. "Thank you for all your sympathy, uncle."

"My boy, there is One above," raising his hand reverently, "who has more pity for us than we have for one another. He can keep him in peace yet. Don't forget that, Charles."

To my office, then, and the morning letters. Amidst them lay Lord Level's answer. Some of its contents surprised me.

Marshdale House,

Tuesday Evening.

> DEAR CHARLES,
>
> If you like to undertake the arrangement of the visit you propose, do so. I have no objection. For some little time

now I have thought that it might be better that my wife should know the truth. You see she is, and has been, liable to hear it at any moment through some untoward revelation, for which she would not be prepared; and the care I have taken to avoid this has not only been sometimes inconvenient to myself, but misconstrued by Blanche. When we were moving about after our marriage, I kept her in unfrequented places, as far as I could, to spare her the chance of this; men's lips were full of it just then, as you know. Blanche resented that bitterly, putting it all down to some curious purposes of my own. Let her hear the truth now. I am not on the spot to impart it to her myself, and shall be glad if you will do so. Afterwards you can take her to see the invalid. I am sorry for what you say of his state. Tell him so: and that he has my sympathy and best wishes.

Blanche has been favouring me lately with some letters written in anything but a complimentary strain. One that I received this morning coolly informs me that she is about to 'Take immediate steps to obtain a formal separation, if not a divorce.' I am not able to travel to London and settle things with her, and have written to her to tell her to come here to me. The fact is, I am ill. Strange to say, the same sort of low fever which attacked me when I was at Marshdale last autumn has returned upon me now. It is not as bad as it was then, but I am confined to bed. Spare the time to bring Blanche down, there's a good fellow. I have told her that you will do so. Come on Thursday if convenient to you, and remain the night. She shall hear what I have to say to her; after that, she can talk of a separation if she likes. You shall hear it also.

Ever truly yours,
LEVEL.

Whilst deliberating upon the contents of this letter, and how I could best carry out its requests, Lennard came in, as usual on his arrival for the day, to give me his report of Tom Heriot. There was not any apparent change in him, he said, either for the better or the worse. I informed Lennard of what I had just heard from the Serjeant.

Then I despatched a clerk to Gloucester Place with a note for Blanche, telling her I should be with her early in the evening, and that she must not fail to be at home, as my business was important.

Twilight was falling when I arrived. Blanche sat at one of the windows in the drawing-room, looking listlessly into the street in the fading light. Old Mrs. Guy, who was staying with her, was lying on the dining-room sofa, Blanche said, having retired to it and fallen asleep after dinner.

How lovely Blanche looked; but how cross! She wore a pale blue silk, her favourite colour, with a gold necklace and open bracelets, from which drooped a heart set with sapphires and diamonds; and her fair, silken hair looked as if she had been impatiently pushing it about.

"I know what you have come for, Charles," she said in fretful tones, as I sat down near her. "Lord Level prepared me in a letter I received from him this morning."

"Indeed!" I answered lightly. "What did the preparation consist of?"

"I wrote to him," said Blanche. "I have written to him more than once, telling him I am about to get a separation. In answer, my lord commands me down to Marshdale"—very resentfully—"and says you are to take me down."

"All quite right, Blanche; quite true, so far. But——"

"But I don't know that I shall go. I think I shall not go."

"A wife should obey her husband's commands."

"I do not intend to be his wife any longer. And you cannot wish me to be, Charles; you ought not to wish it. Lord Level's conduct is simply shameful. What right has he to stay at Marshdale—amusing himself down there?"

"I fancy he cannot help staying there at present. Has he told you he is ill?"

She glanced quickly round at me.

"Has he told *you* that he is so?"

"Yes, Blanche; he has. He is too ill to travel."

She paused for a moment, and then tossed back her pretty hair with a scornful hand.

"And you believed him! Anything for an excuse. He is no more ill than I am, Charles; rely upon that."

"But I am certain——"

"Don't go on," she interrupted, tapping her dainty black satin slipper on the carpet; a petulant movement to which Blanche was given, even as a child.

"If you have come for the purpose of whitening my husband to me, as papa is always doing. I will not listen to you."

"You will not listen to any sort of reasoning whatever. I see that, my dear."

"Reasoning, indeed!" she retorted. "Say sophistry."

"Listen for an instant, Blanche; consider this one little item: I believe Lord Level to be ill, confined to his bed with low fever, as he tells me; you refuse to believe it; you say he is well. Now, considering that he expects us both to be at Marshdale to-morrow, can you not perceive how entirely, ridiculously void of purpose it would be for him to say he is seriously ill if he is not so?"

"I don't care," said my young lady. "He is deeper than any fox."

"Blanche, my opinion is, and you are aware of it, that you misjudge your husband. Upon one or two points I *know* you do. But I did not come here to discuss these unpleasant topics—you are in error there, you see. I came upon a widely different matter: to disclose something to you that will very greatly distress you, and I am grieved to be obliged to do it."

The words changed her mood. She looked half frightened.

"Oh!" she burst forth, before I had time to say another word. "Is it my husband? You say he is ill! He is not dead?"

"My dear, be calm. It is not about your husband at all. It is about some one else, though, who is very ill—Tom Heriot."

Grieved she no doubt was; but the relief that crept into her face, tone and attitude proved that the one man was little to her compared with the other, and that she loved her husband yet with an impassioned love.

By degrees, softening the facts as much as possible, I told the tale. Of Tom's apprehension about the time of her marriage; his trial which followed close upon it; his conviction, and departure for a penal settlement; his escape; his return to England; his concealments to evade detection; his illness; and his present state. Blanche shivered and cried as she listened, and finally fell upon her knees, and buried her face in the cushions of the chair.

"And is there *no* hope for him, Charles?" she said, looking up after a while.

"My dear, there is no hope. And, under the circumstances, it is happier for him to die than to continue to live. But he would like to see you, Blanche."

"Poor Tom! Poor Tom! Can we go to him now—this evening?"

"Yes; it is what I came to propose. It is the best time. He———"

"Shall I order the carriage?"

The interruption made me laugh. My Lord Level's state carriage and powdered servants at that poor fugitive's door!

"My dear, we must go in the quietest manner. We will take a cab as we walk along, and get out of it before turning into the street where he is lying. Change this blue silk for one of the plainest dresses that you have, and wear a close bonnet and a veil."

"Oh, of course; I see. Charles, I am too thoughtless."

"Wait an instant," I said, arresting her as she was crossing the room. "I must return for a moment to our controversy touching your husband. You complained bitterly of him last year for secluding you in dull, remote parts of the Continent, and especially for keeping you away from England. You took up the notion, and proclaimed it to those who would listen to you, that it was to serve his own purposes. Do you remember this?"

"Well?" said Blanche timidly, her colour coming and going as she stood with her hands on the table. "He did keep me away; he did seclude me."

"It was done out of love for you, Blanche. Whilst your heart felt nothing but reproach for him, his was filled with care and consideration for you; where to keep you, how to guard you from hearing of the disgrace and trouble that had overtaken your brother. *We* knew—I and Mr. Brightman—Lord Level's motive; and Major Carlen knew. I believe Level would have given years of his life to save you from the knowledge always and secure you peace. Now, Blanche, my dear, as you perceive that, at least in that one respect, you misjudged him then, do you not think you may be misjudging him still?"

She burst into tears. "No, I don't think so," she said. "I wish I could think so. You know that he maintains some dreadful secret at Marshdale; and that—that—wicked Italians are often staying there—singers perhaps; I shouldn't wonder; or ballet-dancers—anyway, people who can have no right and no business to be there. You know that one of them stabbed him—Oh yes, she did, and it was a woman with long hair."

"I do not know anything of the kind."

"Charles, you look at me reproachfully, as if the blame lay with me instead of him. Can't you see what a misery it all is for me, and that it is wearing my life away?" she cried passionately, the tears falling from her eyes. "I would rather *die* than separate from him, if I were not forced to it by the goings on at that wretched Marshdale. What will life be worth to me, parted from him? I look forward to it with a sick dread. Charles, I do indeed; and now, when I know—what—is perhaps—coming——"

Blanche suddenly crossed her arms upon the table, hid her face upon them, and sobbed bitterly.

"What is perhaps coming?"

"I'm afraid it is, Charles."

"But what is?"

"An heir, perhaps."

It was some moments before I took in the sense of the words. Then I laughed.

"Oh well, Blanche! Of course you ought to talk of separation with *that* in prospect! Go and put your things on, you silly child: the evening is wearing away."

And she left the room.

Side by side on the sofa, Blanche's fair head pillowed upon his breast, his arm thrown round her. She had taken off her bonnet and mantle, and was crying quietly.

"Be calm, my dear sister. It is all for the best."

"Tom, Tom, how came you to do it?"

"I didn't do it, my dear one. That's where they were mistaken. I should be no more capable of doing such a thing than you are."

"Then why did they condemn you—and say you were guilty?"

"They knew no better. The guilty man escaped, and I suffered."

"But why did you not tell the truth? Why did you not accuse him to the judge?"

"I told the judge I was innocent; but that is what most prisoners say, and it made no impression on him," replied Tom. "For the rest, I did not understand the affair as well as I did after the trial. All had been so hurried; there was no time for anything. Yes, Blanche, you may at least take this solitary bit of consolation to your heart—that I was not guilty."

"And that other man, who was?" she asked eagerly, lifting her face. "Where is he?"

"Flourishing," said Tom. "Driving about the world four-in-hand, no doubt, and taking someone else in as he took me."

Blanche turned to me, looking haughty enough.

"Charles, cannot anything be done to expose the man?" she cried. Tom spoke again before I could answer.

"It will not matter to me then, one way or the other. But, Charley, I do sometimes wish, as I lie thinking, that the truth might be made known and my memory cleared. I was reckless and foolish enough, heaven knows, but I never did that for which I was tried and sentenced."

Now, since we had been convinced of Tom Heriot's innocence, the question whether it would be possible to clear him before the world had often been in my mind. Lake and I had discussed it more than once. It would be difficult, no doubt, but it was just possible that time might place some advantage in our hands and open up a way to us. I mentioned this now.

"Ay, difficult enough, I dare say," commented Tom. "With a hundred barriers in the way—eh, Charley?"

"The chief difficulty would lie, I believe, in the fact you acknowledged just now, Tom—your own folly. People argue—they argued at the time—that a young man so reckless as you were would not stick at a trifle."

"Just so," replied Tom with equanimity. "I ought to have pulled up before, and—I did not. Well; you know my innocence, and now Blanche knows it, and Level knows it, and old Carlen knows it; you are about all that are near to me; and the public must be left to chance. There's one good man, though, I should like to know it, Charles, and that's Serjeant Stillingfar."

"He knows it already, Tom. Be at ease on that score."

"Does *he* think, I wonder, that my memory might ever be cleared?"

"He thinks it would be easier to clear you than it would be to trace the guilt to its proper quarter; but the one, you see, rests upon the other. There are no proofs, that we know of, to bring forward of that man's guilt; and——"

"He took precious good care there should be none," interrupted Tom. "Let Anstey alone for protecting himself."

"Just so. But—I was going to say—the Serjeant thinks you have one chance in your favour. It is this: The man, Anstey, being what he is, will probably fall into some worse crime which cannot be hidden or hushed up. When conviction overtakes him, he may be induced to confess that it was he, and not Captain Heriot, who bore the lion's share in that past exploit for which you suffered. Rely upon this, Tom—should any such chance of clearing your memory present itself, it will not be neglected. I shall be on the watch always."

There was silence for a time. Tom was leaning back, pale and exhausted, his breath was short, his face gray, wan and wasted.

"Has Leah been to see you?" Blanche asked him.

"Yes, twice; and she considers herself very hardly dealt by that she may not come here to nurse me," he replied.

"Could she not be here?"

I shook my head. "It would not be safe, Blanche. It would be running another risk. You see, trouble would fall upon others as well as Tom, were he discovered now: upon me, and more especially upon Lennard."

"They would be brought to trial for concealing me, just as I was brought to trial for a different crime," said Tom lightly. "Our English laws are comprehensive, I assure you, Blanche. Poor Leah says it is cruel not to let her see the end. I asked her what good she'd derive from it."

Blanche gave a sobbing sigh. "How can you talk so lightly, Tom?"

"Lightly!" he cried, in apparent astonishment. "I don't myself see very much that's light in that. When the end is at hand, Blanche, why ignore it?"

She turned her face again to him, burying it upon his arm, in utmost sorrow.

"Don't, Blanche!" he said, his voice trembling. "There's nothing to cry for; nothing. My darling sister, can't you see what a life mine has been for months past: pain of body, distress and apprehension of mind! Think what a glorious change it will be to leave all this for Heaven!"

"Are you *sure* of going there, dear?" she whispered. "Have you made your peace?"

Tom smiled at her. Tears were in his own eyes.

"I think so. Do you remember that wonderful answer to the petition of the thief on the cross? The promise came back to him at once, on the instant: 'Verily, I say unto thee, To-day shalt thou be with Me in Paradise.' He had been as much of a sinner as I, Blanche."

Blanche was crying softly. Tom held her to him.

"Imagine," he said, "how the change must have broken on that poor man. To pass from the sorrow and suffering of this life into the realms of Paradise! There was no question as to his fitness, you see, or whether he had been good or bad; all the sin of the past was condoned when he took his humble appeal to his Redeemer: 'Lord, remember me when Thou comest into Thy kingdom!' Blanche, my dear, I know that He will also remember me."

CHAPTER XI.
DOWN AT MARSHDALE.

IT was Thursday morning, the day on which Blanche Level was to travel to Marshdale. She sat in her dining-room at Gloucester Place, her fingers busy over some delicate fancy-work, her thoughts divided between the sad interview she had held with Tom Heriot the previous night, and the forthcoming interview with her husband; whilst her attention was partially given to old Mrs. Guy, who sat in an easy-chair by the fire, a thick plaid shawl on her shoulders and her feet on the fender, recounting the history of an extraordinary pain which had attacked her in the night. But as Mrs. Guy rarely passed a night without experiencing some extraordinary pain or other, Blanche listened absently.

"It is the heart, my dear; I am becoming sure of that," said the old lady. "Last year, if you remember, the physician put it down to spleen; but when I go to him tomorrow and tell him of this dreadful oppression, he will change his opinion."

"Don't you think you keep yourself too warm?" said Blanche, who looked so cool and fresh in her pretty morning dress. "That shawl is heavy, and the fire is warm; yet it is still quite summer weather."

"Ah, child, you young people call it summer weather all the year round if the sun only shines. When you get to be my age, Blanche, you will know what cold means. I dare say you'll go flying off to Marshdale this afternoon in that gossamer dress you have on, or one as thin and flowing."

"No, I shan't," laughed Blanche; "it would be tumbled and spoilt by the time I got there. I shall go in that pretty new gray cashmere, trimmed with silk brocade."

"That's a lovely dress, child; too good to travel in. And you tell me you will be back to-morrow. I don't think that very likely, my dear———"

"But I intend to be," interrupted Blanche.

"You will see," nodded the old lady. "When your husband gets you there, he will keep you there. Give my love to him, Blanche, and say I hope he will be in town before I go back to Jersey. I should like to see him."

Blanche was not paying particular attention to this message. Her attention was attracted by a telegraph boy, who seemed to be approaching the door. The next moment there was a loud knock, which made Mrs. Guy start. Blanche explained that it was a telegram.

"Oh, dear," cried the old lady. "I don't like telegrams; they always give me a turn. Perhaps it's come from Jersey to say my house is burned down."

The telegram, however, had come from Marshdale. It was addressed to Lady Level, and proved to be from her husband.

> *"Do not come to Marshdale to-day. Put it off until next week. I am writing to you. Wait for letter. Let Charles know."*

Now my Lady Level, staring at the message, and being in chronic resentment against her husband, all sorts of unorthodox suspicions rife within her, put the worst possible construction upon this mandate.

"I *knew* how much he would have me at Marshdale!" she exclaimed in anger, as she tossed the telegram on the table. "'Don't come down till next week! Wait for letter!' Yes, and next week there'll come another message, telling me I am not to go at all, or that he will be back here. It *is* a shame!"

"But what is it?" cried old Mrs. Guy, who did not understand, and knew nothing of any misunderstanding between Blanche and her husband. "Not to go, you say? Is his lordship ill?"

"Oh, of course; very ill, indeed," returned Blanche, suppressing the scorn she felt.

Putting the telegram into an envelope, she addressed it to me, called Sanders, and bade him take it at once to my office. He did so. But I had also received one to the same effect from Lord Level, who, I suppose, concluded it best to send to me direct. Telling Sanders I would call on Lady Level that evening, I thought no more about the matter, and was glad, rather than otherwise, that the journey to Marshdale was delayed. This chapter, however, has to do with Blanche, and not with me.

Now, whether the step that Lady Level took had its rise in an innocent remark made by Mrs. Guy, or whether it was the result of her own indignant feeling, cannot be told. "My dear," said the old lady, "if my husband were ill, I should go to him all the more." And that was just what Blanche Level resolved to do.

The previous arrangement had been that she should drive to my office, to save me time, pick me up, and so onwards to Victoria Station, to take the four o'clock train, which would land us at Marshdale in an hour.

"My dear, I thought I understood that you were not going to Marshdale; that the telegram stopped you," said Mrs. Guy, hearing Blanche give orders for the carriage to be at the door at a quarter past three to convey her to Victoria, and perceiving also that she was making preparations for a journey.

"But I intend to go all the same," replied Blanche. "And look here, dear Mrs. Guy, Charles has sent me word that he will call here this evening. When he comes, please give him this little note. You won't forget?"

"Not I, child. Major Carlen is always telling me I am silly; but I'm not silly enough to forget messages."

The barouche waited at the door at the appointed time, and Lady Level was driven to Victoria, where she took train for Marshdale. Five o'clock was striking out from Lower Marshdale Church when she arrived at Marshdale Station.

"Get out here, miss?" asked the porter, who saw Lady Level trying to open the door.

"Yes."

"Any luggage?"

"Only this bag," replied Lady Level.

The man took charge of it, and she alighted. Traversing the little roadside station, she looked to where the fly generally stood; but no fly was there. The station-master waited for her ticket.

"Is the fly not here?" she inquired.

"Seems not," answered the master indifferently. But as he spoke he recognised Lady Level.

"I beg your pardon, my lady. The fly went off with some passengers who alighted from the last up-train; it's not back yet."

"Will it be long, do you know?"

"Well—I —— James," he called to the porter, "where did the fly go to?"

"Over to Dimsdale," replied the man.

"Then it won't be back for half an hour yet, my lady," said the station-master to Lady Level.

"Oh, I can't wait all that time," she returned, rather impatiently. "I will walk. Will you be good enough to send my bag after me?"

"I'll send it directly, my lady."

She was stepping from the little platform when a thought struck her, and she turned to ask a question of the station-master. "Is it safe to cross the fields now? I remember it was said not to be so when I was here last."

"On account of Farmer Piggot's bull," replied he. "The fields are quite safe now, my lady; the bull has been taken away."

Lady Level passed in at the little gate, which stood a few yards down the road, and was the entrance to the field-way which led to Marshdale House. It was a warm evening, calm and sunny; not a leaf stirred; all nature seemed at rest.

"What will Archibald say to me?" she wondered, her thoughts busy. "He will fly into a passion, perhaps. I can't help it if he does. I am determined now to find out why I am kept away from Marshdale and why he is for ever coming to it. This underhand work has been going on too long."

At this moment, a whistle behind her, loud and shrill, caused her to turn. She was then crossing the first field. In the distance she espied a boy striding towards her: and soon recognised him for the surly boy, Sam Doughty. He carried her bag, and vouchsafed her a short nod as he came up.

"How are you, Sam?" she asked pleasantly.

"Didn't think about its being you," was Sam's imperturbable answer, as he walked on beside her. "When they disturbs me at my tea and says I must go right off that there same moment with a passenger's bag for Marshdale House, I took it to be my lord's at least."

"Did they not let you finish your tea?" said Lady Level with a smile.

"Catch 'em," retorted Sam, in a tone of resentment. "Catch 'em a letting me stop for a bite or a sup when there's work to do; no, not if I was starving for 't. The master, he's a regular stinger for being down upon a fellow's work, and t'other's a——I say," broke off Mr. Sam, "did you ever know a rat?—one what keeps ferreting his nose into everything as don't concern him? Then you've knowed James Runn."

"James Runn is the porter, I suppose?" said Lady Level, much amused.

"Well, he is, and the biggest sneak as ever growed. What did he go and do last week? We had a lot o' passengers to get off by the down train to Dover, the people from the Grange it were, and a sight o' trunks. I'd been helping to stow the things in the luggage-van, and the footman, as he was getting into his second-class carriage, holds out a shilling, open handed. I'd got my fingers upon it, I had, when that there James Runn, that rascally porter, clutches hold of it and says it were meant for him, not for me. I wish he was gone, I do!"

"The bull is gone, I hear," remarked Lady Level.

"Oh, he have been gone this long time from here," replied the boy, shifting the bag from one shoulder to the other. "He took to run at folks reg'lar, he did; such fun it were to hear 'em squawk! One old woman in a red shawl he took and tossed. Mr. Drewitt up at the House interfered then, and told Farmer Piggot the bull must be moved; so the farmer put him over yonder on t'other side his farm into the two-acre meadow, which haven't got no right o' way through it. I wish he had tossed that there James Runn first and done for him!" deliberately avowed Sam, again shifting his burden.

"You appear to find that bag heavy," remarked Lady Level.

"It's not that heavy, so to say," acknowledged the surly boy; "it's that I be famishing for my tea. Oh, that there Runn's vicious, he is!—a sending me off when I'd hardly took a mouthful!"

"Well, I could not carry it myself," she said laughingly.

"*He* might ha' brought it; he had swallowed down his own tea, he had. It's not so much he does—just rushes up to the doors o' the trains when they comes in, on the look out for what may be give to him, making believe he's letting folks in and out o' the carriages. I see my lord give him a shilling t'other day; that I did."

"When my lord arrived here, do you mean?"

"No, 'twarn't that day, 'twere another. My lord comes on to the station asking about a parcel he were expecting of. Mr. Noakes, he were gone to his dinner, and that there Runn answered my lord that he had just took the parcel to Marshdale House and left it with Mr. Snow. Upon which my lord puts his hand in his pocket and gives him a shilling. I see it."

Lady Level laughed. It was impossible to help it. Sam's tone was so intensely wrathful.

"Do you see much of Lord Level?" she asked.

"I've not see'd him about for some days. It's said he's ill."

"What is the matter with him?"

"Don't know," said Sam. "It were Dr. Hill's young man, Mitcham, I heard say it. Mother sent me last night to Dr. Hill's for her physic, and Mr. Mitcham he said he had not been told naught about her physic, but he'd ask the doctor when he came back from attending upon my Lord Level."

"Is your mother ill?" inquired Sam's listener.

"She be that bad, she be, as to be more fit to be a-bed nor up," replied the boy: and his voice really took a softer tone as he spoke of his mother. "It were twins this last time, you see, and there's such a lot to do for 'em all, mother can't spare a minute in the day to lie by: and father's wages don't go so fur as they did when there was less mouths at home."

"How many brothers and sisters have you?"

"Five," said Sam, "not counting the twins, which makes seven. I be the eldest, and I makes eight. And, if ever I does get a shilling or a sixpence gived me, I takes it right home to mother. I wish them there two twins had kept away," continued Sam spitefully; "mother had her hands full without them. Squalling things they both be."

Thus, listening to the boy's confidences, Lady Level came to the little green gate which opened to the side of the garden at Marshdale House. Sam carried the bag to the front door. No one was to be seen. All things, indoors and out, seemed intensely quiet.

"You can put it down here, Sam," said Lady Level, producing half-a-crown. "Will you give this to your mother if I give it to you?"

"I always gives her everything as is gived to me," returned Sam resentfully. "I telled ye so."

Slipping it into his pocket, the boy set off again across the fields. Lady Level rang the bell gently. Somehow she was not feeling so well satisfied with herself for having come as she felt when she started. Deborah opened the door.

"Oh, my lady!" she exclaimed in surprise, but speaking in a whisper.

"My bag is outside," said Lady Level, walking forward to the first sitting-room, the door of which stood open. Mrs. Edwards met her.

"Dear, dear!" exclaimed the old lady, lifting her hands. "Then Snow never sent those messages off properly after all! My lady, I am sorry you should have come."

"I thought I was expected, Mrs. Edwards, and Mr. Strange with me," returned Blanche coldly.

"True, my lady, so you were; but a telegram was sent off this morning to stop you. Two telegrams went, one to your ladyship and one to Mr. Strange. It was I gave the order from my lord to Snow, and I thought I might as well send one also to Mr. Strange, though his lordship said nothing about it."

"But why was I stopped?" questioned Blanche.

"On account of my lord's increased illness," replied Mrs. Edwards. "He grew much worse in the night; and when Mr. Hill saw how it was with him this morning, he said your ladyship's visit must be put off. Mr. Hill is with him now."

"Of what nature is his illness?"

"My lady, he has not been very well since he came down. When he got here we remarked that he seemed low-spirited. In a few days he began to be feverish, and asked me to get him some lemonade made. Quarts of it he drank: cook protested there'd be a failure of lemons in the village. 'It is last year's fever back again,' said his lordship to me, speaking in jest. But, strange to say, he might as well have spoken in earnest, for it turns out to be the same sort of fever precisely."

"Is he very ill?"

"He is very ill indeed to-day," answered Mrs. Edwards. "Until this morning it was thought to be a light attack, no danger attending it, nor any symptom of delirium. But that has all changed, and this afternoon he is slightly delirious."

"Is there—danger?" cried Blanche.

"Mr. Hill says not, my lady. Not yet, at all events. But—here he is," broke off Mrs. Edwards, as the doctor's step was heard. "He will be able to explain more of the illness to your ladyship than I can."

She left the room as Mr. Hill entered it. The same cheerful, hearty man that Blanche had known last year, with a fine brow and benevolent countenance. Blanche shook hands with him, and he sat down near her.

"So you did not get the telegram," he began, after greeting her.

"I did get it," answered Blanche, feeling rather ashamed to be obliged to confess it. "But I—I was ready, and I thought I would come all the same."

"It is a pity," said Mr. Hill. "You must not let your husband see you. Indeed, the best thing you can do will be to go back again."

"But why?" asked Blanche, turning obstinate. "What have I done to him that he may not see me?"

"You don't understand, child," said the surgeon, speaking in his fatherly way. "His lordship is in a critical state, the disease having manifested itself with alarming rapidity. If he can be kept perfectly calm and still, its progress may be arrested and danger averted. If not, it will assuredly turn to brain-fever and must run its course. Anything likely to rouse him in the smallest degree, no matter whether it be pleasure or pain, must be absolutely kept from him. Only the sight of you might bring on an excitement that might be—well, I was going to say fatal. That is why I suggested to his lordship to send off the telegram."

"You knew I was coming down, then?" said Blanche.

"My dear, I did know; and —— But, bless me, I ought to apologize to your ladyship for my familiarity of speech," broke off the kindly doctor, with a smile.

Blanche answered by smiling too, and putting her hand into his.

"I lost a daughter when she was about your age, my dear; you put me in mind of her; I said so to Mrs. Edwards when you were here last autumn. She was my only child, and my wife was already gone. Well, well! But that's beside the present question," he added briskly. "Will you go back to town, Lady Level?"

"I would rather remain, now I am here," she answered. "At least, for a day or two. I will take care not to show myself to Lord Level."

"Very well," said the doctor, rising. "Do not let him either hear you or see you. I shall be in again at nine to-night."

"Who is nursing him?" asked Blanche.

"Mrs. Edwards. She is the best nurse in the world. Snow, the head gardener, helps occasionally; he will watch by him to-night; and Deborah fetches and carries."

Lady Level took contrition to herself as she sat alone. She had been mentally accusing her husband of all sorts of things, whilst he was really lying in peril of his life. Matters and mysteries pertaining to Marshdale were not cleared up; but—Blanche could not discern any particular mystery to wage war with just now.

Tea was served to her, and Blanche would not allow them to think of dinner. Mrs. Edwards had a room prepared for her in a different corridor from Lord Level's, so that he would not be in danger of hearing her voice or footsteps.

Very lonely felt Blanche when twilight fell, as she sat at the window. She thought she had never seen trees look so melancholy before, and she recalled what Charles Strange had always said—that the sight of trees in the gloaming caused him to be curiously depressed. Presently, wrapping a blue cloud about her head and shoulders, she strolled out of doors.

It was nearly dark now, and the overhanging trees made it darker. Blanche strolled to the front gate and looked up and down the road. Not a soul was about; not a sound broke the stillness. The house behind her was gloomy enough; no light to be seen save the faint one that burnt in Lord Level's chamber, whose windows faced this way; or a flash that now and then appeared in the passages from a lamp carried by someone moving about.

Blanche walked up and down, now in this path, now in that, now sitting on a bench to think, under the dark trees. By-and-by, she heard the front door open and someone come down the path, cross to the side path, unlock the small door that led into the garden of the East Wing and enter it. By the very faint light remaining, she thought she recognised John Snow, the gardener.

She distinctly heard his footsteps pass up the other garden; she distinctly heard the front door of the East Wing open to admit him, and close again. Prompted by idle curiosity, Blanche also approached the little door in the wall, found it shut, but not locked, opened it, went in, advanced to where she had full view of the wing, and stood gazing up at it. Like the other part of the house, it loomed out dark and gloomy: the upper windows appeared to have outer bars before them; at least, Blanche thought so. Only in one room was there any light.

It was in a lower room, a sitting-room, no doubt. The lamp, standing on the centre table, was bright; the window was thrown up. Beside it sat someone at work; crochet-work, or knitting, or tatting; something or other done with the fingers. Mrs. Snow amusing herself, thought Blanche at first; but in a moment she saw that it was not Mrs. Snow. The face was dark and handsome, and the black hair was adorned with black lace. With a sensation as of some mortal agony rushing and whirling through her veins, Lady Level recognised her. It was Nina, the Italian.

Nina, who had been the object of her suspicious jealousy; Nina, who was, beyond doubt, the attraction that drew her husband to Marshdale; and who, as she fully believed, had been the one to stab him a year ago!

Blanche crept back to her own garden. Finding instinctively the darkest seat it contained, she sat down upon it with a faint cry of despair.

CHAPTER XII.
IN THE EAST WING.

WHAT will not a jealous and angry woman do? On the next morning (Friday) Blanche Level, believing herself to be more ignominiously treated than ever wife was yet, despatched a couple of telegrams to London, both of them slightly incomprehensible. One of the telegrams was to Charles Strange, the other to Arnold Ravensworth; and both were to the same effect—they must hasten down to Marshdale to her "protection" and "rescue." And Mr. Ravensworth was requested to bring his wife.

"She will be some little countenance for me; I'm sure I dare not think how I must be looked upon here," mentally spoke my Lady Level in her glowing indignation.

Lord Level was better. When Mr. Hill paid his early visit that Friday morning, he pronounced him to be very much better; and John Snow said his lordship had passed a quiet night. "If we can only keep him tranquil to-day and to-night again, there will be no further danger from the fever," Mr. Hill then observed to Lady Level.

The day went on, the reports from the sick-room continuing favourable: my lord was lying tranquil, his mind clear. My lady, down below, was anything but tranquil: rather she felt herself in a raging fever. In the evening, quite late, the two gentlemen arrived from London, not having been able to come earlier. Mrs. Ravensworth was not with them; she could not leave her delicate baby. Lady Level had given orders for chambers to be prepared.

After they had partaken of refreshments, which brought the time to ten o'clock, Lady Level opened upon her grievances—past and present. Modest and reticent though her language still was, she contrived to convey sundry truths to them. From the early days of her marriage she had unfortunately had cause to suspect Lord Level of disloyalty to herself and of barefaced loyalty to another. Her own eyes had seen him more than once with the girl called Nina at Pisa; had seen him at her house, sitting side by side with her in her garden smoking and talking—had heard him address her by her Christian name. This woman, as she positively knew, had followed Lord Level to England; this woman was harboured at Marshdale. She was in the house now, in its East Wing. She, Blanche, had seen her there the previous evening.

Mr. Ravensworth's severe countenance took a stern expression as he listened; he believed every word. Charles Strange (I am not speaking just here in my own person) still thought there might be a mistake somewhere. He could not readily take up so bad an opinion of Lord Level, although circumstances did appear to tell against him. His incredulity irritated Blanche.

"I will tell you, then, Charles, what I have never disclosed to mortal man," she flashed forth, in a passionate whisper, bending forward her pretty face, now growing whiter than death. "You remember that attack upon Lord Level last autumn. You came down at the time, Arnold——"

"Yes, yes. What about it?"

"It was that woman who stabbed him!"

Neither spoke for a moment. "Nonsense, Blanche!" said Mr. Strange.

"But I tell you that it was. She was in night-clothes, or something of that kind, and her black hair was falling about her; but I could not mistake her Italian face."

Mr. Ravensworth did not forget Lady Level's curious behaviour at the time; he had thought then she suspected someone in particular. "Are you *sure?*" he asked her now.

"I am sure. And you must both see the danger I may be in whilst here," she added, with a shiver. "That woman may try to stab me, as she stabbed him. She must have stabbed him out of jealousy, because I—her rival—was there."

"You had better quit the house the first thing in the morning, Lady Level, and return to London," said Mr. Ravensworth.

"That I will not do," she promptly answered. "I will not leave Marshdale until these shameful doings are investigated; and I have sent for you to act on my behalf and bring them to light. No longer shall the reproach be perpetually cast upon me by papa and Charles Strange, that I complain of my husband without cause. It is my turn now."

That something must be done, in justice to Lady Level, or at least attempted, they both saw. But what, or how to set about it, neither of them knew. They remained in consultation together long after Blanche had retired to rest.

"We will go out at daybreak and have a look at the windows of this East Wing," finally observed Mr. Ravensworth.

Perhaps that was easier said than done. With the gray light of early morning they were both out of doors; but they could not find any entrance to the East Wing. The door in the wall of the front garden was locked; the entrance gates from the road were locked also. In the garden at the back—it was more of a wilderness than a garden—they discovered a small gate in a corner. It was completely overgrown with trees and shrubs, and had evidently not been used for years and years. But the wood had become rotten, the fastenings loose; and by their united strength they opened it.

They found themselves in a very large space of ground indeed. Grass was in the middle, quite a field of it; and round it a broad gravel walk. Encompassing all on three sides rose a wide bank of shrubs and overhanging trees. Beyond these again was a very high wall. On the fourth side stood the East Wing, high and gloomy. Its windows were all encased with iron bars, and the lower windows were whitened.

Taking a survey of all this, one of them softly whispering in surprise, Mr. Ravensworth advanced to peer in at the windows. Of course, being whitened, he had his trouble for his pains.

"It puts me in mind of a prison," remarked Charles Strange.

"It puts me in mind of a madhouse," was the laconic rejoinder of Mr. Ravensworth.

They passed back through the gate again, Mr. Ravensworth turning to take a last look. In that minute his eye was attracted to one of the windows on the ground floor. It opened down the middle, like a French one, and was being shaken, apparently with a view to opening it—and if you are well acquainted with continental windows, or windows made after their fashion, you may remember how long it has taken you to shake a refractory window before it will obey. It was at length effected, and in the opening, gazing with a vacant, silly expression through the close bars, appeared a face. It remained in view but a moment; the window was immediately closed again, Mr. Ravensworth thought by another hand. What was the mystery?

That some mystery did exist at Marshdale, apart from any Italian ladies who might have no fair right to be there, was pretty evident. At breakfast the gentlemen related this little experience to Blanche.

Madame Blanche tossed her head in incredulity. "Don't be taken in," she answered. "Windows whitened and barred, indeed! It is all done with a view to misleading people. She was sitting at the *open* window at work on Thursday night."

After breakfast, resolved no longer to be played with, Blanche proceeded upstairs to Mr. Drewitt's rooms, her friends following her, all three of them creeping by Lord Level's chamber-door with noiseless steps. His lordship was getting better quite wonderfully, Mrs. Edwards had told them.

The old gentleman, in his quaint costume, was in his sitting-room, taking his breakfast alone. Mrs. Edwards took her meals anywhere, and at any time, during her lord's illness. Hearing strange footsteps in the corridor, he rose to see whose they were, and looked considerably astonished.

"Does your ladyship want me?" he asked, bowing.

"I—yes, I think I do," answered Lady Level. "Who keeps the key of that door, Mr. Drewitt?" pointing to the strong oaken door at the end of the passage.

"I keep it, my lady."

"Then will you be kind enough to unlock it for me? These gentlemen wish to examine the East Wing."

"The East Wing is private to his lordship," was the steward's reply, addressing them all conjointly. "Without his authority I cannot open it to anyone."

They stood contending a little while: it was like a repetition of the scene that had been enacted there once before; and, like that, was terminated by the same individual—the surgeon.

"It is all right, Mr. Drewitt." he said; "you can open the door of the East Wing; I bear you my lord's orders. I am going in there to see a patient," he added to the rest.

The steward produced a key from his pocket, and put it into the lock. It was surprising that so small a key should open so massive a door.

They passed, wonderingly, through three rooms *en suite*: a sitting-room, a bedroom, and a bath-room. All these rooms looked to the back of the house. Other rooms there were on the same floor, which the visitors did not touch upon. Descending the staircase, they entered three similar rooms below. In the smaller one lay some garden-tools, but of a less size than a grown man in his strength would use, and by their side were certain toys: tops, hoops, ninepins, and the like. The middle room was a sitting-room; the larger room beyond had no furniture, and in that, standing over a humming-top, which he had just set to spin on the floor, bent the singular figure of a youth. He had a dark, vacant face, wild black eyes, and a mass of thick black hair, cut short. This figure, a child's whip in his hand, was whipping the top, and making a noise with his mouth in imitation of its hum.

Half madman, half idiot, he stood out, in all his deep misfortune, raising himself up and staring about him with a vacant stare. The expression of Mr.

Ravensworth's face changed to one of pity. "Who are you?" he exclaimed in kindly tones. "What is your name?"

"Arnie!" was the mechanical answer, for brains and sense seemed to have little to do with it; and, catching up his top, he backed against the wall, and burst into a distressing laugh. Distressing to a listener; not distressing to him, poor fellow.

"Who is he?" asked Mr. Ravensworth of the doctor.

"An imbecile."

"So I see. But what connection has he with Lord Level's family?"

"He is a connection, or he would not be here."

"Can he be—be—a son of Lord Level's?"

"A son!" interposed the steward, "and my lord but just married! No, sir, he is not a son, he is none so near as that; he is but a connection of the Level family."

The lad came forward from the wall where he was standing, and held out his top to his old friend the doctor. "Do, do," he cried, spluttering as he spoke.

"Nay, Arnie, you can set it up better than I: my back won't stoop well, Arnie."

"Do, do," was the persistent request, the top held out still.

Mr. Ravensworth took it and set it up again, he looking on in greedy eagerness, slobbering and making a noise with his mouth. Then his note changed to a hum, and he whipped away as before.

"Why is he not put away in an asylum?" asked Mr. Ravensworth.

"Put away in an asylum!" retorted the old steward indignantly. "Where could he be put to have the care and kindness that is bestowed upon him here? Imbecile though he is, madman though he may be, he is dear to me and my sister. We pass our lives tending him, in conjunction with Snow and his wife, doing for him, soothing him: where else could that be done? You don't know what you are saying, sir. My lord, who received the charge from his father, comes down to see him: my lord orders that everything should be done for his comfort. And do you suppose it is fitting that his condition should be made public? The fact of one being so afflicted is slur enough upon the race of Level, without its being proclaimed abroad."

"It was he who attacked Lord Level last year?

"Yes, it was; and how he could have escaped to our part of the house will be a marvel to me for ever. My sister says I could not have slipped the bolt of the passage door as usual, but I know I did bolt it. Arnie had been restless that day; he has restless fits; and I suppose he could not sleep, and must have risen from his bed and come to my sitting-room. On my table there I had left my pocket-knife, a new knife, the blades bright and sharp; and this he must have picked up and opened, and found his way with it to my lord's chamber. Why he should have attacked him, or anyone else, I know not; he never had a ferocious fit before."

"Never," assented Mr. Hill, in confirmation.

Mr. Drewitt continued: "He has been imbecile and harmless as you see him now, but he has never disturbed us at night; he has, as I say, fits of restlessness when he cannot sleep, but he is sufficiently sensible to ring a bell communicating with Snow's chamber if he wants anything. If ever he has rung, it has been to say he wants meat."

"Meat!"

The steward nodded. "But it has never been given to him. He is cunning as a fox; they all are; and were we to begin giving him food in the middle of the night we must continue to do it, or have no peace. Eating is his one enjoyment in life, and he devours everything set before him—meat especially. If we have any particular dainty upstairs for dinner or supper, I generally take him in some. Deborah, I believe, thinks I eat all that comes up, and sets me down for a cannibal. He has a hot supper every night. About a year ago we got to think it might be better for him to have a lighter one, and we tried it for a week; but he moaned and cried all night long for his hot meat, and we had to give it him again. The night this happened we had veal cutlets and bacon, and he had the same. He asked for more, but I would not give it; perhaps that angered him, and he mistook my lord for me. Mr. Hill thought it might be so. I shall never be able to account for it."

The doctor nodded assent; and the speaker went on:

"His hair was long then, and he must have looked just like a maniac when the fit of fury lay upon him. Little wonder that my lady was frightened at the sight of him. After he had done the deed he ran back to his own room; I, aroused by the commotion, found him in his bed. He burst out laughing when he saw me: 'I got your knife, I got your knife,' he called out, as if it were a feat to be proud of. His movements must have been silent and stealthy, for Snow had heard nothing."

At this moment there occurred an interruption. The Italian lady approached the room with timid, hesitating steps, and peeped in. "Ah, how do you do, doctor?" she said in a sweet, gentle voice, as she held out her hand to Mr.

Hill. Her countenance was mild, open, and honest; and a conviction rushed on the instant into Blanche's mind that she had been misjudging that foreign lady.

"These good gentlepeople are come to see our poor patient?" she added, curtseying to them with native grace, her accent quite foreign. "The poor, poor boy," tears filling her eyes. "And I foretell that this must be my lord's wife!" addressing Blanche. "Will she permit a poor humble stranger to shake her by the hand for her lord's sake—her lord, who has been so good to us?"

"This lady is sister to the unfortunate boy's mother," said the doctor, in low tones to Blanche. "She is a good woman, and worthy to shake hands with you, my lady."

"But who was his father?" whispered Blanche.

"Mr. Francis Level; my lord's dead brother."

Her countenance radiant, Blanche took the lady's hand and warmly clasped it. "You live here to take care of the poor lad," she said.

"But no, madam. I do but come at intervals to see him, all the way from Pisa, in Italy. And also I have had to come to bring documents and news to my lord, respecting matters that concern him and the poor lad. But it is over now," she added. "The week after the one next to come, Arnie goes back with me to Italy, his native country, and my journeys to this country will be ended. His mother, who is always ill and not able to travel, wishes now to have her afflicted son with her."

Back in the other house again, after wishing Nina Sparlati good-day, the astonished visitors gathered in Mr. Drewitt's room to listen to the tale which had to be told them. Mrs. Edwards, who was awaiting them, and fonder of talking than her brother, was the principal narrator. Blanche went away, whispering to Charles Strange that she would hear it from him afterwards.

"We were abroad in Italy," Mrs. Edwards began: "it is many years ago. The late lord, our master then, went for his health, which was declining, though he was but a middle-aged man, and I and my brother were with him, his personal attendants, but treated more like friends. The present lord, Mr. Archibald, named after his father, was with us—he was the second son, not the heir; the eldest son, Mr. Level—Francis was his name—had been abroad for years, and was then in another part of Italy. He came to see his father when we first got out to Florence, but he soon left again. 'He'll die before my lord,' I said to Mr. Archibald; for if ever I saw consumption on a man's face, it was on Mr. Level's. And I remember Mr. Archibald's answer as if it was but yesterday: 'That's just one of your fancies, nurse: Frank tells me he has looked the last three years as he looks now.' But I was right, sir; for shortly after that we received news of the death of Mr. Level; and then Mr. Archibald was the heir. My lord, who had grown worse instead of better, was very ill then."

"Did the late lord die in Italy?" questioned Mr. Ravensworth.

"You shall hear, sir. He grew very ill, I say, and we thought he would be sure to move homewards, but he still stayed on. 'Archibald likes Florence,' he would say, 'and it's all the same to me where I am.' 'Young Level stops for the *beaux yeux* of the Tuscan women,' the world said—but you know, sir, the world always was censorious; and young men will be young men. However, we were at last on the move; everything was packed and prepared for leaving, when there arrived an ill-favoured young woman, with some papers and a little child, two years old. Its face frightened me when I saw it. It was, as a child, what it is now as a growing man; and you have seen it today," she added in a whisper. "'What is the matter with him?' I asked, for I could speak a little Italian. 'He's a born natural, as yet,' she answered, 'but the doctors think he may outgrow it in part.' 'But who is he? what does he do here?' I said. 'He's the son of Mr. Level,' she replied, 'and I have brought him to the family, for his mother, who was my sister, is also dead.' 'He the son of Mr. Level!' I uttered, knowing she must speak of Mr. Francis. 'Well, you need not bring him here: we English do not recognise chance children.' 'They were married three years ago,' she coolly answered, 'and I have brought the papers to prove it. Mr. Level was a gentleman and my sister not much above a peasant; but she was beautiful and good, and he married her, and this is their child. She has been dying by inches since her husband died; she is now dead, and I am come here to give up the child to his father's people.'"

"Was it true?" interrupted Mr. Strange.

"My lord thought so, sir, and took kindly to the child. He was brought home here, and the East Wing was made his nursery——"

"Then that—that—poor wretch down there is the true Lord Level!" interrupted Mr. Ravensworth.

"One day, when my lord was studying the documents the woman had left," resumed Mrs. Edwards, passing by the remark with a glance, "something curious struck him in the certificate of marriage; he thought it was forged. He showed it to Mr. Archibald, and they decided to go back to Italy, leaving the child here. All the inquiries they made there tended to prove that, though the child was indeed Mr. Francis Level's, there had been no marriage, or semblance of one. All the same, said my lord, the poor child shall be kindly reared and treated and provided for: and Mr. Archibald solemnly promised his father it should be so. My lord died at Florence, and Mr. Archibald came back Lord Level."

"And he never forgot his promise to his father," interposed the steward, "but has treated the child almost as though he were a true son, consistent with his imbecile state. That East Wing has been his happy home, as Mr. Hill can testify: he has toys to amuse him, the garden to dig in, which is his favourite pastime; and Snow draws him about the paths in his hand-carriage on fine days. It is a sad misfortune, for him and for the family; but my lord has done his best."

"It would have been a greater for my lord had the marriage been a legal one," remarked Mr. Ravensworth.

"I don't know that," sharply spoke up the doctor. "As an idiot I believe he could not inherit. However, the marriage was not a legal one, and my lord is my lord. The mother is not dead; that was a fabrication also; but she is ill, helpless, and is pining for her son; so now he is to be taken to her; my lord, in his generosity, securing him an ample income. It was not the mother who perpetrated the fraud, but the avaricious eldest sister. This sister, the one you have just seen, is the youngest; she is good and honourable, and has done her best to unravel the plot."

That was all the explanation given to Mr. Ravensworth. But the doctor put his arm within that of Charles Strange, and took him into the presence of Lord Level.

"Well," said his lordship, who was then sitting up in bed, and held out his hand, "have you been hearing all about the mysteries, Charles?"

"Yes," smiled Mr. Strange. "I felt sure that whatever the mystery might be, it was one you could safely explain away if you chose."

"Ay: though Blanche did take up the other view and want to cut my head off."

"She was your own wife, your *loving* wife, I am certain: why not have told her?"

"Because I wanted to be quite sure of certain things first," replied Lord Level. "Listen, Charles: you have my tale to hear yet. Sit down. Sit down, Hill. How am I to talk while you stand?" he asked, laughing.

"When we were in Paris after our marriage a year ago, I received two shocks on one and the same morning," began Lord Level. "The one told me of the trouble Tom Heriot had fallen into; the other, contained in a letter from Pisa, informed me that there *had been a marriage* after all between my brother and that girl, Bianca Sparlati. If so, of course, that imbecile lad stood between me and the title and estate; though I don't think he could legally inherit. But I did not believe the information. I felt sure that it was another invented artifice of Annetta, the wretched eldest sister, who is a grasping intriguante. I started at once for Pisa, where they live, to make inquiries in person: travelling by all sorts of routes, unfrequented by the English, that my wife might not hear of her brother's disgrace. At Pisa I found difficulties: statements met me that seemed to prove there had been a marriage, and I did not see my way to disprove them. Nina, a brave, honest girl, confessed to me that she doubted them, and I begged of her, for truth and right's sake, to help me as far as she could. I cannot enter into details now, Strange; I am not strong enough for it; enough to say that ever since, nearly a whole year, have I been trying to ferret out the truth: and I only got at it a week ago."

"And there was no marriage?"

"Tell him, Hill," said Lord Level, laughing.

"Well, a sort of ceremony did pass between Francis Level and that young woman, but both of them knew at the time it was not legal, or one that could ever stand good," said the doctor. "Now the real facts have come to light. It seems that Bianca had been married when very young to a sailor named Dromio; within a month of the wedding he sailed away again and did not return. She thought him dead, took up her own name again and went home to her family; and later became acquainted with Francis Level. Now, the sailor has turned up again, alive and well———"

"The first husband!" exclaimed Charles Strange.

"If you like to call him so," said Mr. Hill; "there was never a second. Well, the sailor has come to the fore again; and honest-hearted Nina travelled here from Pisa with the news, and we sent for his lordship to come down and hear it. He was also wanted for another matter. The boy had had a sort of fit, and I feared he would die. My lord heard what Nina had to tell him when he arrived; he did not return at once to London, for Arnie was still in danger, and he waited to see the issue. Very shortly he was taken ill himself, and could not get away. It was good news, though, about that resuscitated sailor!" laughed the doctor, after a pause. "All's well that ends well, and my Lord Level is his own man again."

Charles Strange sought an interview with his sister—as he often called her—and imparted to her these particulars. He then left at once for London with Mr. Ravensworth. Their mission at Marshdale was over.

Lord Level, up and dressed, lay on a sofa in his bedroom in the afternoon. Blanche sat on a footstool beside him. Her face was hidden upon her husband's knee and she was crying bitter tears.

"Shall you ever forgive me, Archibald?"

He was smiling quietly. "Some husbands might say no."

"You don't know how miserable I have been."

"Don't I! But how came you to fall into such notions at first, Blanche? To suspect me of ill at all?"

"It was that Mrs. Page Reid who was with us at Pisa. She said all sorts of things."

"Ah!"

"*Won't* you forgive me, Archibald?"

"Yes, upon condition that you trust me fully in future. Will you, love?" he softly whispered.

She could not speak for emotion.

"And the next time you have a private grievance against me, Blanche, tell it out plainly," he said, as he held her to him and gave her kiss for kiss.

"My darling, yes. But I shall never have another."

CHAPTER XIII.
CONCLUSION.

I CHARLES STRANGE, took up this story at its commencement, and I take it up now at its close.

It was a lovely day at the end of summer, in the year following the events recorded in the last chapter, and we were again at Marshdale House.

The two individuals who had chiefly marred the peace of one or another of us in the past were both gone where disturbance is not. Poor Tom Heriot was mouldering in his grave near to that in which his father and mother lay, not having been discovered by the police or molested in any way; and the afflicted Italian lad had died soon after he was taken to his native land. Mr. Hill had warned Nina Sparlati that, in all probability, he would not live long. Mrs. Brightman, I may as well say it here, had recovered permanently; recovered in all ways, as we hoped and believed. The long restraint laid upon her by her illness had effected the cure that nothing else might have been able to effect, and re-established the good habits she had lost. But Miss Brightman was dead; she had not lived to come home from Madeira, and the whole of her fortune was left to Annabel. "So you can live where you please now and go in for grandeur," Arthur Lake said to me and my wife. "All in good time," laughed Annabel; "I am not yet tired of Essex Street."

And now we had come down in the sunny August weather when the courts were up, to stay at Marshdale.

You might be slow to recognise it, though. Recalling the picture of Marshdale House as it was, and looking at it now, many would have said it could not be the same.

The dreary old structure had been converted into a light and beautiful mansion. The whitened windows with their iron bars were no more. The disfiguring, unnaturally-high walls were gone, and the tangled shrubs and weeds, the overgrowth of trees that had made the surrounding land a wilderness, were now turned into lovely pleasure-grounds. The gloomy days had given place to sunny ones, said Lord Level, and the gloomy old structure, with its gloomy secrets, should be remembered no more.

Marshdale was now their chief home, his and his wife's, with their establishment of servants. Mr. Drewitt and Mrs. Edwards had moved into a pretty dwelling hard by; but they were welcomed whenever they liked to go to the house, and were treated as friends. The steward kept the accounts still, and Mrs. Edwards was appealed to by Blanche in all domestic difficulties. She rarely appeared before her lady but in her quaint gala attire.

We were taking tea out of doors at the back of the renovated East Wing. The air bore that Sabbath stillness which Sunday seems to bring: distant bells, ringing the congregation out of church, fell melodiously on the ear. We had been idle this afternoon and stayed at home, but all had attended service in the morning. Mr. Hill had called in and was sitting with us. Annabel presided at the rustic tea-table; Blanche was a great deal too much occupied with her baby-boy, whom she had chosen to have brought out: a lively young gentleman in a blue sash, whose face greatly resembled his father's. Next to Lord Level sat my uncle, who had come down for a week's rest. He was no longer Serjeant Stillingfar; but Sir Charles, and one of her Majesty's judges.

"Won't you have some tea, my dear?" he said to Blanche, who was parading the baby.

By the way, they had named him Charles. Charles Archibald; to be called by the former name: Lord Level protested he would not have people saying Young Archie and Old Archie.

"Yes, Blanche," said he, taking up the suggestion of the judge. "Do let that child go indoors: one might think he was a new toy. Here, I'll take him."

"Archibald need not talk," laughed Blanche, looking after her husband, who had taken the child from her and was tossing it as he went indoors. "He is just as fond of having the baby as I am. Neither need you laugh, Mr. Charles," turning upon me; "your turn will come soon, you know."

Leaving the child in its nursery in the East Wing, Lord Level came back to his place; and we sat on until evening approached. A peaceful evening, promising a glorious sunset. An hour after midday, when we had just got safely in from church, there had been a storm of thunder and lightning, and it had cleared the sultry air. The blue sky above, flecked with gold, was of a lovely rose colour towards the west.

"The day has been a type of life: or of what life ought to be," suddenly remarked Mr. Hill. "Storm and cloud succeeded by peace and sunshine."

"The end is not always peaceful," said Lord Level.

"It mostly is when we have worked on for it patiently," said the judge. "My friends, you may take the word of an old man for it—that a life of storm and trouble, through which we have struggled manfully to do our duty under God, ever bearing on in reliance upon Him, must of necessity end in peace. Perhaps not always perfect and entire peace in this world; but assuredly in that which is to come."

THE END.

Milton Keynes UK
Ingram Content Group UK Ltd.
UKHW031926221024
2303UKWH00004B/278